CU00796837

Please Visit the Website at:
http://www.speakquebec.com

Cover illustration: Éric Godin

Speak Québec
ISBN-13: 978-0615986906

© 2006, 2013 Daniel Kraus. All Rights Reserved.
Legal Deposit: September 2006

Library and Archives Canada

Printed in Canada

For Mom and Dad…
Who always taught
that the only true boundries
between cultures are those
we ourselves create.

Thanks

Sincere thanks to the following persons, without whom this book could not have been created:

Michel Besner, Yves Boudreault, la famille Brossart-Galley (Chantal, Jean-François, Anne-Lise, et Églantine), Corinne et Francis Prévote, Martin Chouinard, Thérèse Bruno, Claude Cajolet, Michel Collet, Virginia Crabbé, Nancy Daoust, Eva Dawson, François DesRochers, François du Monthier, François Dunn, Nicholas Ericson, Martin Faucher, Paul & Stacey Ford & family, Eric Godin, Claudia Goyette, Amélie Hébert, Jean-Jacques Hermans, Marie-Claude Hudon, Nina Jones, Peter Kreutlein, Jean Lachance, Luc Laprise, Jacques Larue-Langlois, Laurent Lauzon, Sébastien Lavier, Christian Lavoie, Éric Lebel, Lyne Michaud, Sandra LeMieux, Isabelle LeMieux, Caroline Lévesque, Raymond Lévesque et famille, Raya Mileva, Nancy Nadeau, Sammy Nelson, Ann Nickner, Francois Perusse, Scott Rafer, Manuel Rochon, Michael Sheasby & family, Greg Smith & Diane Laflamme, Michael-David Smith & family, Elisabeth Starenkyj, Steven Tabac, Lisa & Michael Taylor & family, Carol Swedlow, Pierre Toussignant, Josée Tremblay, Marie-Josée Turcotte, Raphael Van Lierop, Keiko Watanabe, Sophie Vincelette and Tami Weinberg.

Special thanks to André Gauthier, Alain Laferrière, and Sébastien Lavier, whose corrections, thoughts, and ideas contributed significantly to this work.

Table of Contents

Forward

This third edition of *Speak Québec* is truly a milestone. With over four thousand copies in print, what began as a handy list for friends has now grown into a well-known reference to the Québec language. For some – largely Francophone readers – this book provides an interesting (and often amusing) source of insight into English. For English-speaking readers, this book has proven an important tool for understanding and communicating at work and in social situations.

The interest that people have taken in *Speak Québec* has been an enormous factor in its growth and success. Since publishing the first edition in 2000, I've received countless emails and letters from both visitors and residents of Québec, offering suggestions, insights, encouragement, and thanks. For this, I am deeply grateful.

In this third edition, we strove to include as many of these contributions and ideas as possible. Most significantly, this edition includes an entirely new chapter – dedicated to helping understand many of the common, colloquial phrases heard on a daily basis around the Province.

Through the years spent working on this book, I have grown ever more amazed by the richness and evolution of the Québec language. While many of its terms and ideas you'll find herein are rooted in Québec's rural history, the language itself continues to grow with a depth and color that is a credit to the Québec culture. The humor and frankness of the Québec people truly shines through in the pages that follow.

My sincere hope is that this 3rd Edition — the result of almost fifteen years of work, research, and discussion — continues to open the doors of Québec culture to visitors, residents, and amateurs of Québec and her language.

Dan Kraus
Montréal, Québec
October 2013

Introduction

Although many works have been published in recent years to help French speakers better understand the many unique words and expressions found in Québec, almost no such resources exist to help English speakers. As any English Canadian or American visitor to the Province du Québec will tell you, the dizzying array of words and phrases particular to the region creates an almost insurmountable barrier to communicating in French – even for those with a strong command of vocabulary and grammar.

The daily language heard in Québec can actually be thought of as a 'superset' of International French – Quebecers comfortably use most French words, but also supplant them with several thousand additional words and colloquialisms of their own. While French-speakers worldwide often joke about the great differences between their spoken and written languages, nowhere is this more in evidence than Québec – few of the thousands of differences from International French heard in conversation are ever written down. Quebecers proudly point out that a good percentage of this rich, textured language comes from *le vieux Français* – Old French – brought here by the first settlers. This is complemented by a number of words adopted both from the Inuit (indigenous northern peoples) and the Native Americans, and also from modern English. These influences combine to form a language that retains all the expansive and artistic nuances found in International French, but is endowed with the rich cultural detail and informality of North-American English as well.

Speak Québec! is designed to be used by English speakers as a practical handbook for understanding Québécois – the day-to-day French spoken in Québec. It is also highly valuable for francophones who wish to understand the English equivalents of common colloquialisms. Although by no means a dictionary of officially-recognized "Canadian French", this book is intended to clearly explain the vocabulary and expressions necessary to speak the rich vernacular found in and around the Province of Québec. In this sense, I deliberately make no judgments herein as to things that are technically or grammatically 'correct', seeking instead to provide the real-world picture of the language needed to understand and appreciate the Québécois culture.

The first part of this work provides a brief history of the Québec language, from its origins in *Nouvelle France* and the Amerindian tongues, to its modern-day influences from English. It also provides a clear explanation of differences in grammar and pronunciation from International French. The second part of the book is a dictionary – a lexicon containing two thousand of the words and phrases most commonly heard throughout the Province, and most necessary for understanding.

The fundamental goal of this book is to open the doors for better communication and cultural exchange between the Québécois people and others, both domestic and abroad. I wish you luck as you unlock the nuances of this tremendously rich and varied language, and hope that this work provides a concrete means of grasping the *joie de vivre* that stands behind one of North America's most unique and undiscovered cultures.

A Brief Linguistic History

Nouvelle-France (... - 1763)

The evolution of the Québec language actually began far before the arrival of the first Europeans. The Native Americans (*Inuit*) who migrated thousands of years before across the Bering Strait developed – unbeknownst to them – many words that survive in daily Québec parlance to this day. The Native Americans – such as the Micmac, the Cree, and the Outaouais – also had a hand in the development of the modern Québec tongue, as their cultures grew and thrived, and as they developed words for the unique world around them.

The arrival of the first French explorer (Jacques Cartier, in 1534) brought French traditions, language, and culture of the period to Québec. Although Cartier made three separate trips to North America – traveling up the St Lawrence river as far south as Montréal – it was only half a century later, with the founding of Québec in 1608 by Samuel de Champlain, that France had a true foothold in the new world. The quickly blossoming fur trade in Québec brought a rising tide of explorers to the province. With the founding of *Ville Marie* (modern-day Montréal) in 1642, French presence in the colonies increased quickly, and the development of the Province of Québec was afoot.

Although the language used in Québec during this period largely reflected the accent of Paris (whence most of the earliest French settlers came), certain regional groups also brought their particular dialects – Normand, Basque, Flemish, etc. Many of the unique accents and linguistic tendencies identified in Québec today date straight back to this period – and the reign of Louis XIV.

As would be expected, however, these new settlers lacked words for many of the things they encountered in their new world. The fauna, flora, and native culture about them had no equivalents even in rural France, and so these early pioneers began to use the native terms for things particular to their new world. Native American words were adopted for modes of transport, and new items (toboggans, moccasins, etc) that had never before been encountered. The same held true for names of new animals (wapiti, caribou), and fish (achigan, ouananiche), who were simply identified by a phonetic transcription of the Native American names. The name *ouaouaron* – giant frog – in fact, derives directly from the Native American onomatopoeia for the deep bellowing sound the creature makes. A good number of city names in Québec were derived from the Native American names for places – towns such as Chicoutimi, Tadoussac, Natashquan, and others. Many other modern Québec terms also evolved from these early days, drawn from agriculture, fishing, and winter survival.

BRITISH CONTROL (1763-1840)

By the mid 18th-century, the gradual arrival of British interests in the new world – and the 13 colonies below – began to have a significant influence on the original French settlers. The inevitable clashes between the two sides began to reflect the almost continuous state of war between their mother countries. The British and French approaches to colonization were notably different, however – whereas the British remained in an essentially urban lifestyle, the French became familiar with the Native Americans, signed treaties with the tribes, and learned their languages. The significant linguistic overlaps with both English and the native tongues increased, and entirely new French words began to appear.

In September of 1759, the armies of British major general James Wolfe and French General Louis Joseph de Montcalm clashed on the Plains of Abraham, just south of the city of Québec. The British victory in this battle, and the fall of the city of Québec to English forces, forever changed the future of *Nouvelle France*. The other major French towns, such as Montréal, surrendered soon after. This victory promulgated the departure of many of the wealthy French and academics; those who did not return to France were on the whole tradesmen, craftsmen, and farmers, who had already put down familial roots in the new world.

Under the Treaty of Paris in 1763, the King of France surrendered the full rights to the territory of Canada to the British Monarchy. This transfer of power opened the doors to a flood of new English-speaking European colonists – who brought with them new ideas, words, and dialects. Many new terms that developed during this period were based on the perception and integration of these new immigrants – words such as *enfirouapé* (a slur of "wrapped in fur") – a pejorative colloquialism for the wealthy English arriving in Quebec City in the post-war years.

Whereas Québec's earliest commerce had been based on fur trading, the evolving social economy of Quebecers began to center increasingly around agriculture. The years that followed the Treaty of Paris were marked by the establishment of the *Seigneurial* system by the British Regime – some 200 separate fiefs of land along the St. Lawrence river, owned by wealthy British landowners, with the land worked principally by the French farmers and tradesmen. These so-called *Habitants* (those who lived and worked on the land) evolved the Québec tongue even further. The harsh winters, and the almost complete dependency on the St. Lawrence River, brought a spirit of strong independence – *un sens debrouillard* – to the culture, and helped evolve a sense of *savoir-faire* that is noticable in Québec even today.

Along with this Seigneural system grew the deep roots of the Catholic theocracy that dominated much of Québec, and its politics, for the century that followed. This religious influence had a marked effect on the language, and brought many religious terms and words into common use.

THE BIRTH OF CANADA (1840-PRESENT)

As the Industrial Revolution sparked the rise of manufacturing, the process of Québec urbanization accelerated, and the previously-rural Francophones began to increasingly answer the call of opportunity close to ports and commerce. By the late 19th century, Montréal had become Canada's premiere industrial center, welcoming also the waves of European immigrants fleeing war in their homelands. Unfortunately, this quick urbanization caused tension between the British and French cultures. English – the traditional language of commerce – was being challenged for the first time as the business language of the province.

The middle of the 20th century marked Québec's transition away from the Catholic theocracy that had effectively ruled its society for a century and a half, and toward a unified and integrated social structure. This "Quiet Revolution" – a sometimes-violent period denoted by a resurgence of pride in Québec's French heritage – marked an increasing Francophone determination to assert their identity, both in Canada and globally. A new sense of unity developed between Francophones, ultimately culminating in the founding of the *Parti Québécois*, and the referedums for the independence of Québec in the years that followed.

The founding of the *Office de la langue Française* in 1961 – a governmental organization instituted to promote use of the French language in the business workplace, and the culture in general – for the first time formalized Québec's intent to define the lingusitic side of its French heritage. In 1969, Pierre Elliot Trudeau's government introduced the *Official Languages Act*, defining both French and English as official languages of Canada, and guaranteed that all government services be made available in both tongues. Québec, on its own initiative, declared itself a bilingual province, and extended these rights at the provincial level as well. In 1977 the Québec government enacted *Bill 101*, declaring French the official language of the province.

Today, the French and English languages co-exist comfortably in Québec. Although French is the official language of the province, many Quebecois are bilingual – communicating freely in both languages.

Pronunciation

The common language spoken in Québec – *Québecois* – is perhaps most typified by its' distinct accent, which is about as different from Parisian French as North American English is from British English. There are about seven major discernable accents throughout the province, ranging from the deep Acadian of the north, to the expansive accent of the Trois-Rivières region, to the curt *patois* spoken near the American border. In general, the further out from the cities you go, the deeper and more historical the accent becomes. A good example of this is the pre-revolutionary "rolled" R sound, which is still heard in some of the more remote regions of Québec.

Sensibly, much of the reason for this historical accent is that the language in Québec did not follow the same evolutionary path as its mother language in France. Modern Québécois is hence a somewhat complicated mix of 16th-century accents combined with tendencies garnered from modern english. There are also many words and phrases that originate directly from accidental slurs of english words and phrases — such as *aldress* (all dressed), *poutine* (put-in), and so on. The resulting language, while pleasing to the ear, can be very difficult to understand. To complicate matters further, Quebecers are reknowned for their tendency to speak very quickly, and often abbreviate or slur words together.

Below we provide an overview of the major differences in pronunciation and grammar between Québécois and International French.

General Pronunciation Tendancies

/a/ becomes /â/ or /ô/

The Québec /a/ is often very deep, and may more or less resemble an /o/ sound:

moi, là → moé, lô
là, je te dis → lô, chte dzi
câlisse → côlisse

/i/ and /è/ become /é/ and /a/

Perhaps the best-known hallmark of the Québec accent, this tendancy directly reflects the standard pronunciation used prior to the French Revolution.

moi → moé
toi → toé
merci → marci
merde → marde
chercher → charcher
couverture → couvart

/e/ becomes /é/

dehors → déhors
bedaine → bédaine
pesant → pésant

/è/ becomes /é/ or /à/

mère → mére; père → pére
frère → frà
j'avais → j'avà
poulet → poulà
vrai → vrà

/ê/ becomes /AY/

fête → f<u>AY</u>te
fève → f<u>AY</u>ve

/u/ becomes /eû/ in front of a consonant

bûche → b<u>eû</u>che
il fume → il f<u>eû</u>me

/i/ often becomes /é/ in front of a consonant

mille → m<u>é</u>lle
pipe → p<u>é</u>pe
risque → r<u>é</u>sque
vite → v<u>é</u>te

/ou/ becomes /ô/ in front of a consonant

courte → c<u>ô</u>rte
il pousse → il p<u>ô</u>sse
toute → t<u>ô</u>te

/in/ becomes a nasal /ain/ at the end of words

chemin → chem<u>ain</u>
jardin → jard<u>ain</u>

/i/ is softer

In general, the /i/ sound is pronounced more softly and quickly:

vite → vit
suite → swit

Slurs

/le/ and /la/ become /l'/

Quebecers often drop the /e/ or /a/ from *le* in front of words that start with a consonant, simply slurring the two consonants together.

Le camion → l'camion
La chandelle → l'chandelle
Le tapis → l'tapis

/u/ becomes /i/, and /ou/ becomes /u/

Deeper vowels, such as /u/ and /ou/ are often replaced with sounds more comfortably produced in the front of the mouth:

bas-culotte → bas-kilotte; député → dépité
soulier → sulier; sous-sol → sus-sol

/j/ pronounced as /ch/

The /j/ sound is often truncated, replaced entirely by a /sh/ or /ch/ sound:

je suis → chwee
justifier → chustifier

/re-/ becomes /ar-/

Quebecers sometimes replace the /re-/ at the beginning of words with /ar-/:

revenir → arvenir
refaire → arfaire

… and often completely drop the vowels /i/, /u/, and /ou/, creating a liaison as necessary with the /z/ sound:

arriver → arver
camisole → camzole
mes idées → mezdees

Affriction

Heard very frequently, affrication is the deliberate addition of an /s/ or /z/ sound after a /t/ or /d/ and a /il/y/ or /u/:

Tu dis → tsu dzi
dur → dzur
peinture → peintsure
tunnel → tsunnel

Dipthongs

Long and nasal vowels are often transformed into dipthongs, providing a more open, and sometimes nasal, sound than in International French:

faire → FAY-yure
banque → bawnque

A particularly frequent case of this is the transformation of /or/ into /aor/:

encore → encaor

Clipped Endings

Quebecers often completely drop the ends of words – especially those ending with /re/ and / le/:

genre → /gen/
article → /arteek/
par exemple → /par examp/

A final /r/ is also often transformed simple into an /é/:

tiroir → tiroé
mouchoir → mouchoé

Verbs & Conjugating

The verbs *être* and *avoir* are pronounced quite differently by Quebecers, and are often almost inaudible in quick speech. Below is a table demonstrating English, International French, and common Québec pronunciations:

Être (to be)

English	Int. French	Québec
I am	je suis	/shui/
You are	tu es	/tay/
He/She/It is	il est	/yay/
	elle est	/elay/
	on est	/onay/
We are	nous sommes	(use "on" form instead)
You (*pl.*) are	vous êtes	/vzêt/
They are	ils sont	/iyson/ elles sont/eson/

Avoir (to have)

English	Int. French	Québec
I have	j'ai	/shé/
You have	tu as	/ta/
He, She, It has	il a	/ya/
	elle a	/ela/
	on a	/ona/
We have	nous avons	(use 'on' form instead)
You (pl.) have	vous avez	/vzavé/
They have	ils ont	/ihyon/
	elles ont	/ezon/

Notable also is the Québec tendency to use the simple future (future proche) almost exclusively, instead of differentiating future events by using the verb aller. For example:

English	Int. French	Québec
I'll go a bit later	*Je vais aller tantôt*	*J'irais tantôt*
You'll see him tomorrow	*Tu vas le voir demain*	*Tu le verra demain*

Structural Differences

There are a vast number of differences between French and common Québec parlance at the structural level. We summarize here the elements requiring explanation that are most frequently heard in daily conversation.

Double Words

Words can often be doubled for increased effect, especially in the negative:

Sa musique n'est pas fort-fort. — His music isn't really that great.
Je l'aimais pas ben-ben. — I wasn't really that fond of it.

English Usage

Quebecers primarily use English to enhance an idea, or to express an extreme. For example:

C'était vraiment bad. – That was really the worst.

This also holds for well-known English phrases which have not really been appropriated into common usage – if the French word seems overly complex, Quebecers will often simply substitute the English word.

Les Autres

Quebecers often replace *nous* with *nous autres*, and *vous* with *vous âutres*. This is similar in style to English "you guys" or "Y'all" rather than just "you". In the *nous* form, it's about the same as "we all".

Nous and Vous

One of the most confusing issues of usage in Québec is with whom to use the *nous* and *vous* forms of verbs. Different from their Gallic cousins, Quebecers are often significantly less formal, and so frequent use of *vous* is often more of a distancing measure than a politeness, especially among young people. As a general rule, introductions are made using the "vous" form – and then people quickly switch to using "tu".

Supressed Articles

The stand-alone particle *à* is often used to replace *ce*, when making reference to a time already familiar in context, such as *à soir* (this evening) or *à matin* (this morning).

When using *à* (meaning "to"), *dans* or *jusqu'à*, the particle following it is often dropped – for example, *à gare* (*à la gare*), *à prochaine* (*à la prochaine*), *dans maison* (*dans la maison*).

Tenses

Quebecers tend to use the conditional very frequently, especially when ordering or asking for something:

Je prend<u>rais</u> le bœuf — ... I'll have the beef (when ordering at a restaurant)

Word-Level Changes

The /tsu/ construct

The addition of /tsu/ causes some of the most complicated combinations in Québécois. At many points in the language, on when asking a question, an additional /tsu/ or /s'tu/ is added. Some of the major idiomatic expressions include:

(Ça) se peut-<u>tsu</u> que... — Could it be that...
<u>t</u>'as-tsu — Do you have...
<u>tu</u> peux-tsu — Can you...
<u>s'tu</u> pour vrai? — Is that for real?

Il and Lui

Québécers often drop particles and pronouns almost completely, or relegate them to their final sound. For example:

Eng.:　　I've often said...
Fr.:　　Je lui ai souvent dit...
Queb.:　*<u>J'y</u> ai souvent dit...*

Eng.:　　There are three.
Fr.:　　*Il y en a trois.*
Queb.:　*<u>Y en</u> a trois.*

Là

Là is used in two different senses — to mean "there" (indicative), and also "now". Often heard is the expression *Là, la* — meaning "As for that…" — or literally, "there, now…"

Ne… pas

In Québécois, either the *ne* or the *pas* can be omitted, and still retain the negative sense of the sentence.

> *Je ne peux répondre au téléphone en ce moment.* — I can't come to the phone right now.
> *Je peux pas répondre au téléphone en ce moment.* — I can't come to the phone right now.

Prepositions québécois

Sentences in are often terminated with prepositions — similar to English:

> *Le gars que je sors avec* — The guy (that) I'm going out with (*sl.*).

rather than:

> *Le gars avec qui je sors* — The guy with whom I'm going out.

Sayings and Slurs

Québécois contains a tremendous number of colloquial sayings – often pronounced with such speed that it's difficult to understand either the words, or root meaning. The lexicon below highlights some of the more popular Québec sayings and slurs, which may frequently be heard in casual conversation, or between friends.

Phonetic Pronunciation	Actual Spelling	Meaning
Aickssa?	Avec ça?	With That?
Anteka	En tout cas	Anyway
Anweille!	Envoye!	Move it!
Astheure	À cette heure	Now, Nowadays
Ben wéyon don!	(et) Bien, voyons donc!	You're kidding!
Cammtoé	Calme-toi	Chill out / Relax
Check-moi le don!	Cheque moi le donc	Look at that guy!
Chu danlune	Je suis dans la lune	I'm spacing out (sl)
Chudans l'marde	Je suis dans la marde	I'm in (deep) shit
Ch'tout fourré	Je suis tout fourré	I'm all mixed up
Chtsedsi (là)	Je te dis, là	I'm tellin' ya...
Drette-là	à droite-là	Right there
Garsa!	Regarde ça!	Check that out!

Phonetic Pronunciation	Actual Spelling	Meaning
Garledon!	Regarde-le donc!	Look at him!
Garladon!	Regarde-la donc!	Look at her!
Kesstufay	Qu'est-ce que tu fais	What's up? What are you doing?
Métonque	Mettons (que)	Let's say that… If it were that…
Mott'were t'aiyeur!	Je vais te voir toute à l'heur!	See ya later!
Pis?	(et) Puis?	And so? What's up?
Sad' lairasah	Ca a l'air à ca	It looks that way
S'tacause que…	C'est à cause que…	It's because…
S'tassé	C'est assez	That'll do That's enough
Tatu d'javu ca?	As-tu déjà vu ca?	Have you ever seen that before?
Tsu m'cré-tu?	Tu me cré-tu?	Can you believe it?
*Vadon chier**!*	Va donc chier**	You're shitting me! (You're kidding)
Vadon toé!	Va donc, toi!	No way! (You're kidding!)

Swears and Insults

Swears and insults (*jurons*) are used with such grace and flair in Québec that they merit a separate chapter to correctly explain their usage and inflection. This chapter includes an overview of the most important words in this more "colorful" part of the Québec tongue, their meanings, and an idea of usage. The reader is advised to use extreme caution with these words, since — as with oaths in English — they can easily offend people in the wrong context.

The Nouns

Most Québec *jurons* are of religious origin, a historical ramification of the strong religious overtones that dominated the society through the 18th and 19th centuries. As such, most of the *jurons* come from objects from and around the ceremony of the Roman Catholic mass.

Baptême : *n.f.* – Baptism.
Câlisse : *n.m.* – Chalice, cup used for receiving wine in the Roman Catholic mass.
Calvaire : *n.m.* – Calvary, place where Christ was crucified.
Ciboire : *n.m.* – Ciborium, dish used for distributing the host in the Roman Catholic mass.
Crisse : *n.m.* – Christ.
Esprit : *n.m.* – Holy Spirit.
Ostie : *n.m.* – Host, body of Christ in the Roman Catholic mass.
Sacrament : *n.m.* – Sacrament.
Saint Chrem : *n.m.* – Chrism (holy oil)
Tabarnac : *n.m.* – Tabernacle, place where the host is kept.
Viarge : *n.f.* – Virgin, reference to the Virgin Mary.

Although each of the *jurons* has a different meaning, they are more or less interchangeable from an expletive point of view — when used independently, they all roughly equivocate "*shit!*" or "*goddam!*" in terms of visceral effect.

Typical examples of uses might include:

Crisse qu'y fait frette! – Shit, it's cold!
Sacrament que ce gars-là est épais! – Goddamit that guy is an idiot!
Câlisse que j'en ai marre! – I've goddam well had it!
Ostie que je suis tanné! – I'm so goddam sick of this!

To express frustration or swear lasciviously, combinations of words are often heard — since they're relatively easy to link together:

Ostie de crisse de Tabarnac!
Ostie de ciboire de calvaire!

The word *ostie* is often addended to sentances for added emphasis, for example:

J'en ai marre, ostie! – I've goddamwell had it!

Additionally, almost any of the nouns can be used in combination with *être* to describe a state of being angry or upset:

être en tabarnac – to be pissed off
être en câlisse – " " " "
être en crisse – " " " "

Là, je suis vraiment en tabarnac! – I'm really pissed off right now!
La conversation qu'on a eue m'a mis en beau calvaire. – The conversation we had left me furious.

The Use of *jurons* with the partitive "en" generally means "a lot of":

J'en ai eu de la bouffe en tabarnac – I had one hell of a lot of food.

There are, of course, almost infinite variations of each of the above words, most used to soften the sound. *Câlisse* and *Tabarnac* are the most often changed to these less-offensive versions, roughly equivocating "*Damn!*" or "*Dammit!*" in English:

Câlisse : Câline, Calif, Caltor.
Tabarnac : Tabarnouche, Tabarouette, Tabarslak, Taboire, Barnak, Tabarnane, Tabarnic, Taburn,

Other frequently-heard *petits jurons* – less offensive variants – include:

Calvâsse
Cibolle
Maudit
Maususse
Mautadine
Mautadit
Jériboire
Simonac
Saint-Gériboire
Saint-Sacrifice
Torrieux

The Adjectives

Almost any of the *jurons* can be used to augment the meaning of a noun, or replace the word *très* (very). Note that the gender of the *juron* is always determined by the word it's modifying:

Ça, c'est <u>une ostie de</u> belle fille ! – That's one damn fine looking girl.
Mon chum est <u>un crisse d'</u>idiot ! – My boyfriend is a goddam idiot!
T'es un criss de cave, toi – You're a real jerk.

Oaths, especially *crisse* and *câlisse*, sound stronger when used to modify a noun, as in the above example, than when standing on their own.

The Verbs

Most *jurons* also have verb equivalents.

Se crisser de (quelque chose); *Se câlisser de (quelque chose)*; *Se tabarnaker de (quelque chose)* — to not give a damn about something.

… and so on. For example:

Je m'en crisse s'il fait froid, je vais quand même aller skier.
I don't give a damn if it's cold, I'm still going skiing.

To increase the effect of the words as verbs even further, the word *contre* to the front of either — *s'en contrecâlisser, s'en contrecrisser*. For example:

Je m'en contrecâlisse s'il vient avec ou non. — I really don't give a shit if he comes along or not.

Both *câlisser* and *crisser* can also indicate direction, in the sense of throwing or projecting something in a careless manner:

Je vais crisser ça dans les vidanges. — I'm gonna throw it the hell out.
Je vais le câlisser dehors s'il continue de même. — I'm gonna throw him the hell out of here if she keeps on like that.

Dictionary

To simplify reference, the dictionary part of this book is structured alphabetically according to general Québécois terms, which are then subdivided into the different ways in which each word is commonly used.

- English words are included herein only when a difference in nuance or usage makes a justified distinction from standard English usage, or when the frequency of their use makes their importance worth noting. Words which are essentially equivalent in both languages, such as car parts (*dash*, etc.), or words adopted directly from English (*brunch*, *shack)* are not included.

- Words included that are International French are denoted by a preceding *Fr.* Such French vocabulary is generally included to help indicate the difference between the Québécois language nuance and that of International French, or to highlight words which are used with uncommon frequency in Québec. The reader should bear in mind that in day-to-day language words are often used in both the International French meaning and that particular to Québec, depending on the context. For example, *partir* – which in International French means simply "to leave", can mean "to leave" *or* "to start" in Québécois.

- Italicized phrases following an entry serve as examples of usage. Those phrases offset with a dot, "❧", are idioms or phrases commonly heard in conversation.

- Stars are used to denote strong or offensive terms. A single star (★) indicates something which is a bit impolite, a double star (★★) indicates something rude, and a triple star (★★★) indicates something extremely rude or vulgar which should be avoided.

Due to the frequency of contractions of International French found in Québec parlance (for example, *ben* rather than *bien*, *betôt* rather than *bientôt*, etc), we have included herein phonetic equivalents of commonly-heard contractions and slurs, to help make them simple to find and understand.

Abbreviations / Conventions Used

angl. – anglicism
cf. – see also
conj. – conjunction
contr. – contraction
Def. – deformation
engl. – English
ex. – example
expl. – expletive
expr. – idiomatic expression
impl.– implies
incl. – including
interj. – interjection
Fr. – International French
Lit. – literally
orig. – origin
pl. – plural
pron. – pronoun
sim. – similar to
sl. – slang
n. – noun
m. – masculine
f. – feminine

A

À : *Prep. − Fr.* to, at, about.

 à l'année longue − the whole year.

à soir − tonight.

à cause ? − why?
À cause t'as fait ça ? − Why did you do that?

à cause (que) − because.
C'est pas d'à cause ! − You're right!

à cette heure (là) − now, at this point. *Lit.* "at this hour".

à cheval (sur les détails) − hung up on the details *Lit.* on horseback for the details.

à date − until now, up to this point.

à l'épouvante − as fast as possible.

à l'instant − now, at (this) time.

à la mitaine − by hand. *Lit.* "by the mitten".

à mort − to the extreme *Lit.* unto death.
Il est pénible à mort. − He's unbelivably annoying.

à part (de) ça − Aside from that, additionally.

à peine − with difficulty.

à pic − irritable, ill-tempered.

(pas) à peu près − really, significantly.
Il est faché, et pas à peu près ! − He's really angry.

À tantôt ! − See you later!

à terre − exhausted, finished, dead. *Lit.* "on the ground".
La batterie dans ma voiture est completement à terre − My car battery is completely dead.

A-1 : *adj.* − top notch, the best. *N.B. Pronounced as in english: /ey whun /.*

(en) Abondance : *n.m.* − a lot (of something).

Abreuvoir : *n.m.* − water fountain, tap.

Abrier : *v.t.* − to cover, to shelter, to protect.

> *As-tu abrié tes rosiers? Ça va geler ce soir.* − Did you cover the rosebushes? It's going to freeze tonight.

Accommodations : *n.f. pl.* − lodging, accommodations.

Accommoder : *v.i.* − 1. to receive, accommodate, host. 2. To help, to accommodate (someone).

> *L'hotel peut accomoder presque milles personnes.* − The hotel can accomodate almost a thousand people

Accomplir : *v.i.* − *Fr.* to accomplish

> ❧ *accomplir mer et monde* − to move heaven and earth, to overcome enormous difficulties. *Lit.* to accomplish heaven and earth.

Accordant(e) : *adj.* − accomodating.

(s') Accorder : *v.t.* − to get along.

> ❧ *s'accorder comme chien et chat* − to fight non-stop. *Lit.* to get along like cats and dogs.

Accotable : *adj.* − easily competed with or defeated.

> *Dans son métier, il n'est pas accotable* − He can't be beaten in his profession.

Accoté(e) : *adj.* − hooked, attached.

> *Je suis un homme accoté.* − I'm an attached man.
> ❧ *être accoté* − to live together (out of wedlock).

Accoter : *v.t.* − 1

Accoter : *v.i.* – 1. to push or lay against. 2. to compete with, to challenge. 3. to attain the same level as (the competition).

Acccote-toi sur moi, ca va brasser ! – Hang on to me, this is gonna be rough!

Accoucher : *v.i.* – to give birth.

🌿 *Accouche qu'on baptise !* – Get on with it! *Lit.* Give birth so we can baptize! Often only the first word is used, and the rest understood : « *Accouche !* »

Accrocher : *v.t.* – *Fr.* to hang up. 2. to run into, to collide with.

🌿 *accrocher ses patins* – to end one's career, give up. *Lit.* to hang up [one's] skates.

(d') Accoutumée : *adv.* – typically, usually.

D'Accountumée, il arrive vers cinq heures. – Typically, he arrives around five o'clock.

Accroire : *v.t.* – believe. *Def. Fr.* 'croire'.

Accroire : *n.m.* – belief.

🌿 *faire des accroires* – to make (someone) believe something untrue, to decieve someone.
Elle m'avait fait des accroires qu'elle était experte, mais enfin du compte elle n'en était pas du tout. – She had made me believe that she was an expert, but in the end she wasn't at all.

Accoutumance : *n.m.* – habit, custom.

Achalandé(e) : *adj.* – congested, crowded.

La rue était trop achalandée pour faire du vélo. – The road was too congested to go bike-riding.

Achalage : *n.m.* − annoyance, nonsense.

Achalant(e) : *n.m. /f. & adj.* − (one who is) annoying, bothersome, exasperating.

Achaler : *v.t.* − to harass, to annoy, to disturb.

Acharné : *adj.* − insisting, overly forceful. Used when speaking of people, not objects.

Achever : *v.t.* − to make it to the end, to bring to a conclusion.

> *Il faut qu'il continue à travailler s'il veut achever.* − He needs to keep working if he wants to make it.

Acrage : *n.m.* − acreage, landsize.

Actuellement : *adv.* − currently, presently.

> *La compagnie fait actuellement face à deux défis* − The company is currently facing two challenges.

Adon : *n.m.* − luck, chance.

On s'est croisés par adon. − We happened to bump into each other yesterday.

> *Bien d'adon* − willing to get along, willing to help.
> *Mon prof est bien d'adon quand je lui démande de m'aider avec tout ca* − My professor is really wiling to help when I ask him to give me a hand with that stuff.

Adonnant : *adj.* − likeable, friendly.

Adonner : *v.i.* − 1. to be convenient, to be possible.

On voulait assister à votre soirée, mais ça n'a pas adonné. − We wanted to join in your party, but it just wasn't possible.

(s') Adonner : *v.i.* − 1. to be convenient, to be possible. 2. to get along (well)

Ta mère et moi, on s'adonne bien ensemble.− Your mom and I get along great.

❧ *Ca s'est adonné que…* − It turns out that…

Adresse de retour : *n.m.* − return address (for a letter).

Ad vitam aeternam : *expr.* − without end. *Lit.* to the eternal life. Used to express frustration

Son invité a parlé ad vitam aeternam; on était obligé de quitter avant la fin du souper − His guest talked endlessly; we had to leave before the end of dinner.

Affaire : *n.f.* − 1. thing, item. 2. stuff. 3. issue, problem. 4. business. 5. situation. Not used as *Engl.* "affair", meaning extramarital relationship.

❧ *être en affaire* − to be in business, to be moving along.
❧ *faire affaires* − to do business.
❧ *faire l'affaire* − to be sufficient, to do the job.
   Tiens, du savon va faire l'affaire. − Here, some soap will do the job.
❧ *heures d'affaires* − business hours.
❧ *(un) petit affaire* − a little bit, a hint.
❧ *paquet d'affaires* − bunch of stuff (to do).
❧ *(une) drôle d'affaire* − strange situation.
   Ramasse tes affaires, s'il te plaît, on s'en va. − Get your stuff together, please, we're leaving.
   C'est pas de mon affaire, mais je pense que t'as tort. − It's none of my business, but I think you're wrong.
   C'est une affaire un peu croche. − It's kind of a nasty deal.

Affiler : *v.t.* − to sharpen.

Agace : *n.f.* − *contr.* Agace-pissette.

Agace-pissette★ : *n.f.* – tease (sexual sense).

Agasser : *v.t.* – to bug, to irk, to bother.

Âge d'or : *n.m.* – elderly years. *Lit.* the golden years.

Agneau : *n.m.* – *Fr.* lamb.
* *doux comme un agneau* – very polite, very gentle – usually said of someone very kind. *Lit.* soft as a lamb.

Agrès : *n.m.* – unattractive person.

Aickssa : *expr.* – with that. *Def.* avec ça.

Aiguiller : *v.i.* – to direct, to point (in a direction).
Peux-tu m'aiguiller vers la pharmacie, s'il te plaît ? – Could you point me to to the pharmacy, please?

Aiguiser : *v.t.* – to sharpen.

Aiguisoir : *n.m.*- pencil sharpener.

Aînés : *n.m. pl.* – the elderly.

Ainsi de suite : *conj.* – *Fr.* and so on and so forth.

Air : *n.m.* – 1. *Fr.* air 2. the semblance, the similarity.
* *avoir l'air.* – to seem, to appear.
 Ça a l'air qu'ils y vont quand même. – It seems like they're going anyway.
* *avoir un air de bœuf* – to be in a bad mood.
* *avoir l'air idiot.* – to seem like an idiot.
* *avoir l'air mais pas la chanson.* – to have it in principle, but not in practice. *Lit.* to have the tune but not the song.

Aire de repos : *n.m.* – rest area.

Aisé : *adj.* – easy, in a relaxed sense.

    ❧ *prendre (ça) aisé.* – to take it easy.

Ajouter : *v.i., v.t.* – *Fr.* to add.

    ❧ *ajouter de la job* – to add work (to something)
    ❧ *ajouter en plus* – to add (even more).

Ajuster : *v.t.* – to adjust

Ajustable : *adj.* – adjustable.

Âldresse : *adj.* – with everything (sandwich, pizza, etc). *Def. eng.* all-dressed.

Alentour(s) : *n.masc. pl.* – 1. surroundings, local area. 2. around.

    Est-ce qu'il y a un dépanneur dans les alentours ? – Is there a convenience store around here?
    Il y a plusieurs gamins alentour du char. – There're several kids around the car.

Alldress : *adj.* – with everything. Used in the context of food. *Def. Engl.* all dressed.

    Je prends un hamburger alldress, s'il te plaît. – I'll take a hamburger with everything, please.

Allège : *n.m.* – windowsill.

Aller : *v.i.* – 1. *Fr.* to go. 2. *sl.* to go for, to accept.

    Je vais y aller pour le steak aussi. – I'll go for the steak too.
    ❧ *au pire aller* – in the worst case.
    ❧ *aller au batte* – to go to bat (for something or someone), to step up to the plate, to face an upleasant situation.
    ❧ *aller à l'épouvant* – to go at full speed.
    ❧ *aller à malle* – to go get the mail.
    ❧ *aller aux toasts* – to score, to hit a goal

🎋 *aller aux vues* – to go to the movies.

🎋 *aller virer à…* – to head out to…

Allô : *expr.* – Hello. Often used in the same sense as *Bonjour*, not exclusively on the telephone, as in France.

Allophone : *n.m/f.* – someone whose native tongue is neither french nor english.

Allumé : *adj.* – 1. *Fr.* lit, lighted 2. lit, a bit tipsy. 3. turned on, (sexually) excited.

Allumer : *v.t., v.i.*– 1. *Fr.* to light up, to illuminate. 2. to become clear or lucid. 3. to excite sexually, *sl.* to turn on.

J'ai allumé l'instant qu'il me l'a expliqué. – I understood the moment he explained it to me.
Arrête de m'allumer, toi ! – Stop turning me on!

Allumette : *n.f.* – *Fr.* match

🎋 *gros(se) comme une allumette* – as thin as a matchstick.

Allure : *n.f.* – set of desired qualities, allure.

🎋 *avoir (bien) de l'allure* – to be acceptable, good, valuable.

🎋 *(ne pas) avoir de l'allure* – 1. (of a person) to have bad judgement 2. (of a situation) to make no sense.
Ça n'a pas d'allure, ta situation. – Your situation isn't pretty.

Amanché : *adj.* – 1. set, prepared. 2. stacked (for a girl), well-hung (for a guy).

Amancher : *v.t., v.i.* – to be prepared, to be all set.

Cette affaire-là est super bien amanchée. – That business is really well-prepared.
🎋 *(se) faire amancher* – to be had, to be taken advantage of.
🎋 *mal amanché* – badly off, unprepared.

Amanchage : see *Amanchure.*

Amanchure : *n.f.* – 1. trouble, mess. 2. badly-done work.

   amanchure de broche à foin – badly-organized mess. *Lit.* a haywire mess

Amande : *n.f.* – almond.

   gouter l'amande – to be delicious. *Lit.* 'to taste of almonds'.

Ambitionnant : *adj.* – motivating, stimulating.

Ambitionner : *v.i.* – 1. to exaggerate. 2. to compete.

   ambitionner sur (quelquechose/quelqu'un) – 1. to expect the unreasonable of (something/someone), 2. to take advantage of a situation.
   Moi, je trouve que t'ambitionne bien trop sur ses capacités – I think you're counting way too much on his abilities

(s') Ambitionner : *v.i.* – to work hard, to outdo one's self.

Ambitionneux : *n.m/f.* – ambitious person.

Amen : *interj.* – Amen.

   jusqu'à amen – without end, indefinately.

Amérindien : *n.m. /f., adj.* – Native American.

Ami(e) : *n.m/f.* – *Fr.* friend.

   ami de garçon – friend (male)
   amie de fille – friend (female)
   faire ami(e) (avec quelqu'un) – to become friends (with someone).

(s') Amolir : *v.i.* – to soften.

   Après ces années ensemble, il commence à s'amolir un peu. – After these years together, he's beginning to soften a bit.

Amour : *n.m.* – *Fr.* Love.

❦ *tomber en amour* – to fall in love.

An? : *expr.* – huh?

Ancre : *n.m.* – anchor.

❦ *rester à l'ancre* – to await, remain motionless. *Lit.* 'to remain at anchor'
Elle n'a pas bougé depuis le départ de son mari – elle reste à l'ancre. – She hasn't moved at all since her husband left – she's in the same place.

Ange : *n.m.* – angel

❦ *ange cornu* – one who misrepresents their good intentions. *Lit.* horned angel.
❦ *beau comme un ange* – truly beautiful.

Anglais d'Angleterre : *n.m/f.* – British English (person or language). Use to differentiate from a Canadian Anglophone.

Anglo : *n.m.* – *contr.* anglophone.

Anglophone : *n.m/f* – native English-speaker.

Année : *n.f.* – *Fr.* year.

❦ *à l'année longue* – the whole year.

Anniversaire : *n.f.* – anniversary (marriage, etc.). Note that in Québec the word *fête*, rather than *anniversaire*, is the word generally used for 'birthday'.

Annonce(s) : *n.f. pl.* – com-mercial(s), public message(s).

Je vais y aller pendant les annonces. – I'll go during a commercial.

Anweille (donc)! : *expr.* − *sl.* C'mon! Move your butt! *Def. Envoye donc!*

Anteka : *expr.* − anyhow, in any case. *Def.* En tout cas.

Aouair : *v.t.* − to have. *Def.* avoir.

On va aouair un méchant fun à soir. − We're gonna have a wicked-good time tonight.

Appel : *n.m.* − call, phone call.

  ❋ *(appel) à frais virés* − collect call.
  ❋ *placer un appel* − to place a call.

Applaudissement(s) : *n.m.* − clapping, cheers.

Appliquer : *v.i.* − to apply (for a job, etc)

Apporter : *v.t.* − *Fr.* to bring along.

  ❋ *(pizza) à apporter* − pizza to go.

Apportez votre vin : *expr.* − Bring your (own) wine. Sign typically seen on Québec restaurants which serve food, but have no liquor license.

(pas) Apprenable : *adj.* − (not) able to be learned, (not) easily understood.

Appui-livres : *n.m.* − *pl.* bookends.

Après : *prep.* − 1. after, afterwards. 2. against.

Je vais la voir après. − I'm going to see her afterwards.
Elle est fâchée après lui. − She's mad at him.
  ❋ *par après* − afterwards, next.

Arachide : *n.f.* − peanut.

  ❋ *Beurre d'arachide* − peanut butter.

Aréoport : *n.m.* – Airport. *Def.* 'Aeroport'.

Armoire : *n.f.* – 1. cupboard. 2. closet.

(en) Arracher : *v.t.* –1. to tear, to rip. 2. to have difficulty doing something. 3. to work hard.

Ma sœur en arrache avec son cours d'Anglais. – My sister is really having problems in her English class.

 ❦ *être en arrache* – to be out of money; to be broke.

 ❦ *arracher le cœur* – to be terribly upsetting. *Lit.* 'to tear the heart'.

(s') Arracher : *v.i.* – to defend oneself.

Arranger : *v.t.* – to set up, to arrange.

Je t'ai arrangé un souper avec mon ami. – I set up a dinner for you with my friend.

 ❦ *arranger le cadran (de quelqu'un)* – to beat (someone) up. *Lit.* to set (someone's) alarm clock.

Arrêt : *n.m.* – 1. stop. 2. stop sign. Most Québec stopsigns are uniqely written with *ARRÊT*, rather than STOP.

Arrêt donc! : *expr.* – You're kidding!

Arriver : *v.i.* – *Fr.* to arrive.

 ❦ *arriver comme un chien dans un jeu de quilles* – to come crashing into a situation. *Lit.* to arrive like a dog into a bowling game.

Arsoudre : *v.i.* – *Def. resoudre* (to arrive uninvited)

Arsuer : *v.i.* – to fog up (a mirror, window, etc)

Articulé : *adj.* – articulate. (Used to describe a person).

Arvenir : *v.i.* – *Def. revenir* (to come back).

Arvirer : *v.i.* – *Def. revirer* (to turn around).

Arvoler : *v.i.* – *Def. revoler* (to fly apart).

Assermentation : *n.f.* – swearing-in (ceremony).

(s')Assir : *v.i.* – *Def. s'asseoir* (to sit).

Assurance-Santé : *n.f.* – health insurance. Typically used to denote Québec's privatized health-insurance system.

Astheure : *expr.* – Now, nowadays. *Def.* À cette heure.

Astiner : *v.i.* – *cf.* Ostiner.

Astineux(-euse) : *n.m/f & adj.*– *cf.* Ostineux

Atacas : *n.m. pl.* – cranberry (jelly).

Atchoum : *n.m.* – sneeze.

Atchoumer : *v.i.* – to sneeze. From the onomatopoeia (« *Atchoo!* »).

Atout : *n.m.* – asset.

  ❦ *avoir de l'atout* – to be skilled, to be handy (with something)

Atteignable : *adj.* – attainable, able to be achieved.

Attendre : *v.i.* – *Fr.* to wait, to stay.

  ❦ *attendre aprés (quelqu'un)* – to wait for (someone).
  ❦ *attendre minute* – hold on a sec.
  ❦ *attendre du nouveau* – to be expecting a child; to be pregnant
    Lit. to wait for a new one.

Attention à toi! : *expr.* – Take care of yourself!

Attoquer : *v.i.* – to push against (something).

Attraper : *v.t., v.i.* − *Fr.* to catch.

🌿 *attraper son air* − 1. to catch one's breath 2. to be caught by surprise by something or someone.

Attriquage : *n.m.* − manner of dress.

Mal attriqué : *expr.* − badly dressed.

Au dela (de) : *Fr.* above. More than.

Au juste : *expr.* − anyway, actually.

🌿 *C'est quoi ça, au juste ?* − What is that, anyway?

Aubaine : *n.f.* − sale, discount.

Autant (que) : *adv.* − as much (as).

(En) autant que… − insofar as…

Auto–Patrouille : *n.m.* − patrol car.

Autographier : *v.t.* − to sign, autograph

Autoroute : *n.f.* − highway. Highways in Québec are often referred to simply by their number − *Ex.* « la 40 » (*Autoroute 40*), « *la 112* » (*autoroute 112*), etc.

Autre : *adj.* − *Fr. other, further.* 1. Different, above. 2. More, further.

Il se prend pour quelqu'un d'autre − He believes himsel.f different.
🌿 *… ou autre* − … or something else.

Avancant : *adj.* − Positive, favorable forward-looking *Lit.* Advancing.

Un mec comme lui, pour une fille c'est pas avancant − A guy like that doesn't do a girl good.

Avant-midi : *n.m.* – morning. *Lit.* before-noon.

Avec : 1. *Fr.* with. 2. also.

❦ *Dérangez-vous pas, on va aller avec.* – Don't worry, we'll go also.

Avoir : *v.t., v.i.* – *Fr.* to have.

Il n'y a rien là. – don't sweat it, it's nothing, it's not important.

❦ *(se faire) avoir* – to be had, to be taken advantage of.

❦ *avoir l'air* – to seem.

❦ *avoir l'air de la chienne à Jacques* – to be badly dressed. *Lit.* to seem like Jacques' dog.

❦ *avoir l'air simple* – to make a fool of oneself.

❦ *avoir un air de bœuf* – to be in a bad mood.

❦ *avoir de l'atout* – to be skilled, to be handy (with something)

❦ *avoir du bacon* – to have money, to be wealthy.

❦ *avoir un face de boeuf* – to be in a bad mood. *Lit.* to have a face of beef.

❦ *avoir les baguettes en l'air* – to gesticulate wildly.

❦ *avoir des bébittes* – to have problems/issues. *Lit.* to have bugs.

❦ *avoir des bidous* – to have money, to be rich.

❦ *avoir son biscuit* – 1. to have one's proper compensation. 2. to have scored (in a sexual sense).

❦ *avoir les bleus* – to be down in the dumps, to have the blues.

❦ *avoir sa botte* – to be involved in a sexual relationship.

❦ *avoir la bouche molle* – to slur one's words (most notably, after drinking). *Lit.* 'to have a soft mouth.'

❦ *avoir de la broue dans le toupet* – to have much work to do.

❦ *avoir mal à la cervelle* – to have a headache.

❦ *avoir le cerveau en marmelade* – to be all mixed up. *Lit.* to have jelly for brains.

❦ *avoir du chien* – to have determination or character. *Lit.* to have some dog.

❦ *avoir le gros bout du bâton* – to have the advantage *Lit.* to hold the big end of the stick.

❧ *avoir son char* – to be fed up.

❧ *avoir du chiendent* – to have a lot of character.

❧ *avoir la chienne* – to be afraid, to be worried.

❧ *avoir le cœur dans la gorge* – 1. to be nauseous. 2. to be on the verge of tears. *Lit.* to have one's heart in one's throat.

❧ *avoir la couenne dure* – to be thick-skinned.

❧ *avoir un coup dans le nez* – to have drunk a lot.

❧ *avoir juste le cul et les dents* – 1. to have no personality. 2. to be extremely thin. *Lit.* to have just an ass and teeth.

❧ *avoir le débâcle* – to have the runs, to have diarrhea.

❧ *avoir de l'eau dans la cave* – to wear pants that are too short. *Lit.* "to have water in the cave".

❧ *avoir la coupe rude* – to be in a bad mood. *Lit.* 'to have a rude cut'.

❧ *avoir la face à terre* – to be annoyed, to be vexed.

❧ *avoir la falle basse* – to have a long face, to be down.

❧ *avoir la felle creuse* – to be very hungry.

❧ *avoir de la classe* – to have class, to be educated. Generally used in the negative, to describe someone ("*Pas de classe !*").

❧ *avoir une crotte sur le cœur* – to have a chip on one's shoulder, to be prejudiced against someone.

❧ *avoir le feu au cul*★★ – to be furious. *Lit.* to have fire in one's ass.

❧ *avoir le feu au passage* – to be furious. *Lit.* to have fire in the passage.

❧ *avoir un front de beu* – to be unflappable, to be unshakable. *Lit.* to have the brow of an ox.

❧ *avoir pour son dire que…* – to think that… *Lit.* 'to have for his say (that)…'

❧ *avoir du fun* – to have fun, to have a good time.

❧ *avoir le goût (de faire quelque chose)* – to feel like (doing something).

❧ *avoir des gosses*★ – *sl.* to have balls, to be brave.

❧ *avoir le guedille au nez* – to have a runny nose.

❧ *avoir de la gueule* – to have character, to have a strong presence. *Lit.* to have mouth.

avoir la gueule fendue jusqu'aux oreilles – to be grinning from ear to ear.

avoir du guts – *sl.* to have guts.

avoir des idées croches – to have bad (dishonest) thoughts.

avoir de la jarnigoine – 1. to be a chatterbox, to be overly talkative. 2. to be intelligent.

avoir sa journée dans le corps – to have had a rough day. *Lit.* 'to have (his) day in (his) body.'

avoir un kick sur quelqu'un – to have a crush on someone.

avoir la langue à terre – 1. to be exhausted. 2. to be very hungry. *Lit.* to have (one's) tongue on the ground.

avoir la langue sale – to have a dirty mouth. *Lit.* to have a dirty tongue.

avoir les mains pleines de pouces – to be all thumbs.

avoir la mèche courte – to have a short fuse, to be quick-tempered.

avoir de la mine dans le crayon – to have a ravenous sexual appetite *Lit.* to have lead in the pencil.

avoir de la misère – to have difficulty.

avoir du monde à la messe – to be crowded. *Lit.* "to have people at the Mass"

avoir le moton – to be choked up, to have a lump in one's throat.

avoir le motton – to have bucks, to have money.

avoir le nez brun – to be a brown-noser.

avoir les oreilles dans le crin – 1. to be careful, fearing something or someone. 2. to be in a bad mood. *Lit.* to have one's ears in horse-hair.

avoir les deux pieds dans la même bottine – to be clumsy, unresourceful. *Lit.* to have both feet in the same shoe.

avoir une poignée dans le dos – to be gullible. *Lit.* to have a handle on one's back.

avoir quelque chose pour une chanson – to get something for a song.

🦫 *avoir le sourire fendu jusqu'aux oreilles* – to be smiling from ear to ear.

🦫 *avoir le temps dans sa poche* – to take one's time, to go slowly. *Lit.* to have time in one's pocket.

🦫 *avoir la tête à Papineau* – to be very intelligent. *Lit.* to have the head of Papineau.

🦫 *avoir toute son idée* – to have a clear mind (said of a sharp-minded elderly person).

🦫 *avoir le va-vite* – to have diarrhea. *Lit.* to have the go-quickly.

🦫 *avoir de la visite* – to have guests (over).

🦫 *avoir son voyage* – to have had enough, to be fed up. *Lit.* to have one's trip.

🦫 *avoir vu neiger* – to have experience. *Lit.* to have seen it snow before.

🦫 *avoir vu passer des gros chars* – to have experience. *Lit.* "to have seen big cars go by".

🦫 *avoir des yeux (tout) croches* – to have squinty eyes.

🦫 *avoir les yeux dans le beurre* – to be tired.

🦫 *avoir les deux yeux dans le même trou* – to be exhausted. *impl.* to be staring at a point in space. *Lit.* to have both one's eyes in the same hole.

🦫 *avoir des yeux dans la graisse de bines* – to be glassy-eyed. *Lit.* "to have one's eyes in the bean grease".

🦫 *avoir des yeux pochés* – to have rings around one's eyes.

🦫 *avoir des yeux rond comme des piastres* – to have eyes round like saucers.

🦫 *avoir des yeux tout le tour de la tête* – to have eyes in the back of one's head.

Avoir su... : *expr.* – Had I known...

Ayoye ! : *excl.* – 1. Ouch! 2. Wow!

B

Babillard : *n.m.* − billboard.

Babiche : *n.f.* − animal skin.

   (se) serrer la babiche − to tighten one's belt, to cut down

Baboune : *n.f.* − Fr. lips.

   faire la baboune − to pout.

Backer : *v.t., v.i.* − to back up, support (financially or otherwise).

   On a trouvé quelqu'un pour backer notre nouvelle business. − We found someone to support us in our new business.

Backstore : *n.m.* − storage, backroom.

Bacon : *n.m.* − 1. Bacon, ham. 2. Money, cash.

   Sors ton bacon, ca va coûter cher! − Get out your money, this is going to cost quite a bit!
   avoir du bacon − to have money, to be wealthy.
   se pogner le bacon − to goof off, to do nothing

Bad : *adj.* − *Eng.* (extremely) bad. Used to imply the worst possible case.

   C'est vraiment bad, son problème. − His problem is really the worst.

Badloqué : *adj.* − unlucky.

Bâdrant(e) : *adj.* − annoying, irritating.

Bâdrer : *v.t.* − to bother, annoy.

   Ne me bâdre pas avec tes histoires. − Don't bother me with your tales.

Badtripper : *v.i.* − 1. to flip out, to be distracted 2. to suffer 3. to have a bad trip (drug-related)

> *Elle badtrippe depuis le mort de son père.*− She's been a mess since her dad died.

(se) Baigner : *v.t. /v.i.* − to bathe

> ❊ *baigner dans l'huile* − to go well, to go smoothly. *Lit.* to bathe in oil.

Bagosse : *n.f.* − alcohol, particularly home-distilled alcohol.

Bain : *n.m.* − *Fr.* bath, bathtub.

> ❊ *bain tourbillon* − whirlpool, hottub.

Baiser : *v.i.* − *Fr.* to kiss.

Baise–la–piastre : *n.m /f.* − Miser, greedy person. *Lit.* "Coin-kisser"

Bajoues : *n.f. pl.* − rosy cheeks.

Bal des finissants : *n.m.* − prom.

Balai : *n.m.* − broom.

> ❊ *aller au balai* − to leave someone alone
> ❊ *avoir le balai bas* − to be sad, dejected. *Lit.* 'to have the broom low'.
> ❊ *ballon-balai* − broom-ball. Popular Québec game derived from hockey, played on-foot using brooms and a ball rather than sticks and a puck.
> ❊ *fou comme un balai* − overjoyed, exuberant. *Lit.* crazy as a broom.
> ❊ *jomper le balai* − to become pregnant. *Lit.* 'to hop on the broom.'

Balance : *n.f.* – 1. *Fr.* scale. 2. balance (financial term).

Voici le moitié, je te paierai la balance demain. – Here's half, I'll give you the balance tomorrow.

Balancigner : *v.i.* – to balance on a see-saw.

Les gamins veulent aller balancigner dans le parc – The kids want to to go see-saw in the park.

Balayeuse (électrique) : *n.f.* – vacuum.

Veux-tu passer la balayeuse dans le salon, s'il te plaît ? – Would you vacuum the living room, please?

Ballone : *n.f.* – balloon.

> ❧ *être en balloune* – to be pregnant.
> ❧ *partir sur une balloune* – to go on a bender, to get drunk.
> ❧ *souffler dans la balloune.* – to take a breathalyzer test. *Lit.* to blow in the balloon.

Ballant : *n.f.* – balance, equilibrium.

Balle : *n.f.* – ball. Often used to denote a responsibility, as in English.

Ouais, il m'a passé la balle là-dessus. – Yeah, he passed me the ball on that.

Ballon : *n.m.* – (inflatable) ball.

> ❧ *crever le ballon de quelqu'un* – to burst someone's bubble.
> ❧ *lancer un ballon* – to start a rumor, particularly a political one.

Ballone : *n.f.* – balloon.

> ❧ *être en balloune* – to be pregnant.
> ❧ *partir sur une balloune* – to go on a bender, to get drunk.
> ❧ *péter la balloune* – to fail a breathalyzer (alcohol) test.
> ❧ *peter la balloune (de quelqu'un)* – to burst (someone's) bubble.
> ❧ *souffler dans la balloune* – to take a breathalyzer test. *Lit.* to blow in the balloon.

Baloné : *n.m.* − baloney.

Balustre : *n.m.* − balcony.

Banc de neige : *n.m./expr.* − snowbank.

Bandage★★ : *n.m.* − erection.

Baptême★★ : *excl.* − Shit! ★★ *Lit.* Baptism.

Barbier : *n.m.* − barber (for men).

Barbot : *n.m.* − drawings, markings, graffiti.

Barda : *n.m.* − noise
  ❧ *faire du barda* − to be noisy.

Bardassement : *n.m.* − annoying noise.

Bardasser : *v.i.* − 1. to be pushed, shoved, turned topsy-turvey. 2. to bang around (in anger)

Barfer : *v.i.* − to barf, to throw up.

Barré(e) : *n.m.* − barred, kept out.

  On risque d'être barrés d'ici si tu continues de même. − We are going to be thrown out of here permanently if you keep that up.

Barginer : *v.t.* − to deal, to bargain.

  Il s'est barginé un super de bon deal. − He bargained himself a great deal.

Barniques : *n.f. pl.* − glasses, spectacles.

Barre : *n.f.* − bar.
  ❧ *barre de savon* − bar of soap.

Barré : *adj.* − locked.

Barrer : *v.t.* − to lock.

   As-tu barré la porte ? − Did you lock the door?

Barrure : *n.f.* − lock, deadbolt.

Bas : *adj.*− *Fr.* low.

   en bas de... − below...

Bâs : *n.m.* − socks, stockings.

   manger (ses) bâs − to be uncomfortable with one's speech or action, *sim.* "open mouth, extract foot". *Lit.* to eat one's socks.

Bas–culottes : *n.m. pl.* − panty-hose.

Bassinette : *n.f.* − crib.

(se) Batâiller : *v.i.* − to argue, to dispute.

Bâtisse : *n.f.* − building.

Bâton : *n.m.* − stick, club.

   tenir le gros bout du bâton − to have the advantage *Lit.* to hold the big end of the stick).

Bat : *n.m.* − 1. bat. (baseball). 2. Joint (marijuana)

   aller au bat − to go to bat for something or someone, *i.e.* to face an upleasant situation.

Bavassage : *n.m.* − gossip.

Bavasser : *v.i.* − to gossip, to talk behind someone's back.

Bavasseux (-euse) : *n.m. /f.* − gossipy person.

Baveux, euse : *n. & adj.* – arrogant, annoying, offensive (person)

Bazou : *adj.* – jalopy, heap.

  Aye, c'est un beau bazou, ça! – Hey, nice car!

Beau/belle : *adj.* – *Fr.* beautiful, nice.

  C'est beau. – It's nice/good. Often used in reply to an expression of thanks.

  beau comme un ange – truly beautiful.

  beau smatte – wise-ass, smarty-pants.

Bébé la-la : *n.m.* – one who acts like a child; crybaby.

Bébelle : *n.f.* – 1. toy. 2. thing, small object.

Ramasse tes bébelles, on s'en va, là. – Pick up your toys, we're leaving now.

Bébitte : *n.m.* – insect.

  avoir des bébittes – to have problems/issues.

  bébite à patates – ladybug.

Bec : *n.m.* – small kiss, especially the double-cheek kiss popular in Québec.

  avoir le bec en cul de poule* – to have a continental French accent. Typically refers to someone who retains a French accent, despite several generations of family history in Québec Province. *Lit.* "to have one's face in a hen's bottom".

  bec sucré – sweet tooth.

  faire le bec fin – to be fussy about what one eats.

  se sucrer le bec – to eat, particularly sweets.

Bécosse : *n.f.* – bathroom, toilet. *Contr.* engl. Back-house.

  aller aux bécosses – to go to the bathroom.

Bedaine : *n.f.* − belly, *sl.* gut.

  ❅ *bedaine de bière* − beer-belly.
  ❅ *se promener en bedaine* − to go shirtless.
    Aye, tu commences à avoir une vraie bedaine, là ! − Hey, you're
    starting to get a real gut!

(se) Baigner : *v.t.* − *Fr.* to bathe

  ❅ *baigner dans l'huile* − to go smoothly, to be working okay. *Lit.*
    "to bathe in oil".
  Quant au reste du projet, pour le moment ça baigne dans l'huile − As for
  the rest of the project, for the moment it's going pretty smoothly.

Baril : *n.m.* − *Fr.* barrel.

  ❅ *gros comme un baril* − obese.

Beigne : *n.m.* − doughnut.

Beignerie : *n.f.* − doughnut shop.

Ben : *adj.*, *adv.* − well. *Contr.* bien.

  ❅ *ben-ben* − very.
    Ce n'était pas ben-ben bon, finalement − It wasn't that great, after
    all.
  ❅ ben manque − probably, perhaps.
    On va ben manque aller souper ensemble ce soir − We'll probably
    dine together tonight.

Benefic : *adj.* − beneficial, advantageous.

Bémol : *n.m.* − negative thing, negative idea.

  Il y a juste un petit bémol : Jacques ne vient pas. − There's just one
  negative thing − Jacques won't be coming.

Bécher : *v.t.* − to fall, to trip on something.

Bequer : *v.t.* – to kiss, to give a peck.

Bétail : *n.m.* – 1. beast (of burden). 2. difficult job or task.

❦ *ostie*★★ *de bétail* – a hell of a job.

Bête : *adj.* – rude, impolite.

❦ *avoir l'air bête* – to seem unfriendly.
❦ *faire un air bête* – to look (at someone) with contempt.

Bête puante : *n.m.* – skunk.

Bêtise : *n.f.* – 1. *Fr.* Nonsense, silliness. 2. insult, affront.

Béton : *n.m.* – *Fr.* concrete.

❦ *couler (quelque chose) dans le béton* – to write (something) in stone, to fix something permanently. *Lit.* to pour something in concrete.

Betôt : *adv* – soon (*contr.* bientôt).

Bette : *n.f.* – beet, face.

Lui as-tu vu la bette quand on l'a trouvé ? – Did you see his face when we found him?

Beurrade : *n.f.* – a buttery substance. Used to describe anything that, similar to butter, can be smeared or slathered on something.

Beurre : *n.m.* – *Fr.* butter.

❦ *avoir les yeux dans le beurre* – to be tired.
❦ *beurre de pinotte* – peanut butter.
❦ *pédaler dans le beurre* – to make useless efforts. *Lit.* "to pedal in butter".
❦ *tourner dans le beurre* – to go nowhere. *Lit.* "to turn in butter:

Beurrer : *v.t. – Fr.* to butter, to spread.

 beurrer épais – to lay it on thick, to exaggerate.

 beurrer la face – to show someone up, to rub something in someone else's face.
Jean m'a beurré la face avec son nouveau travail. – Jean rubbed his new job in my face.

Beus : *n.m. pl.* – police, *sl.* cops, pigs. *Contr.* French *bœufs* (steer, oxen).

Biberon : *n.m. – Fr.* baby bottle

 boire comme un biberon – to drink like a fish. *Lit.* to drink like a baby's bottle.

Bibitte : *n.f.* – 1. insect. 2. problem, issue.

 avoir des bibittes – to have problems.
 Bibitte à poil – small animal.
 Bibitte à patates – cockroach.

Bicycle à gaz : *n.m.* – motorcycle.

Bidou : *n.m.* – money.

 avoir des bidous – to have money, to be well-off.
Ca prend des bidous – That costs real money.

Bien-être social : *n.m.* – welfare. Abbreviated as *BS*.

Bienvenue ! : *expr.* – Welcome! Also used in response to "Thanks" ("You're welcome").

(Tax de) Bienvenue : *n.m.* – Welcome Tax. Typically, taxes owed to the Québec Government upon purchase of a new house or condominium.

Bière : *n.f. – Fr.* beer.

- *bière d'épinette* – root beer.
- *bière en fût* – draft beer.
- *bière tablette* – room-temperature beer.
- *être de la petite bière* – to be without importance. *Lit.* to be of small beer.

Bine : *n.f.* – 1. Bean. 2. face.

- *avoir un drôle de bine* – to make a funny face, to make a strange expression.

En goutant sa bière, il a fait un drôle de bine. – When he tasted his beer, he made a funny face.

- *être une bine* – to be nothing, to be small.
- *être rond comme une bine* – to be completely sloshed (drunk). *Lit.* "to be as round as a bean".

Binette : *n.f.* – face.

- *avoir un drôle de binette* – to make a funny face, to make a strange expression.

En goutant sa bière, il a fait un drôle de binette. – When he tasted his beer, he made a funny face.

Binnes : *n.m. pl.* – (baked) beans.

- *avoir des yeux dans la graisse de binnes* – to be glassy-eyed. *Lit.* "to have one's eyes in the bean grease".

A chaque fois qu'il la voit, il a les deux yeux dans la graisse de binnes – Every time he sees her, he get completely distracted.

Binerie : *n.f.* – small, inexpensive restaurant.

Bisouner : *v.i.* – to fiddle.

Biscuit : *n.m. – Fr.* cookie.

- *avoir son biscuit* – 1. to have one's proper compensation. 2. to have scored (in a sexual sense).

Bitcher★★ : *v.t.* – to complain, *sl.* to bitch★★.

Lui, il a bitché là-dessus pendant un bon 10 minutes. – He complained about it for a good 10 minutes.

Bizoune★★ : *n.f.* – sexual organs. Usually male, but occasionally used for the female.

Blanc : *n.m.* – blank (space).

avoir un blanc de mémoire – to draw a blank (speaking of one's memory).

Blanchon : *n.m.* – baby seal.

Blaster : *v.t/v.i.* – to yell at (someone).

Je me suis fait blaster par ma blonde de ne pas avoir apporté des fleurs. – I really caught it from my girlfriend for not bringing flowers.

Blé d'Inde : *n.m.* – corn on the cob. *Lit.* "India wheat"

Bleacher : *v.t.* – to bleach, tint white.

Demain, je vais me bleacher les cheveux. – Tomorrow I'm going to bleach my hair.

Bleu : *n.m.* – 1. bruise. 2. state of being sad.

J'ai toujours quelques bleus de ma randonnée à bicyclette. – I still have a few bruises from my bike trip.

avoir les bleus – to be down in the dumps, to have the blues.

Bleuet : *n.m.* – 1. blueberry. 2. Native of the Saguenay/Lac-Saint-Jean region, well-known for its blueberries.

Blind pig : *expr.* – Speak-easy, illegal barroom.

Bloc : *n.m.* – 1. city block 2. concrete or other support block.

La gare est à trois blocks par là. – The train station is three blocks that way.

Son char est sur les blocs depuis une semaine. – His car has been up on blocks for one week now.

Bloke★★ : *n.m.* – English Canadian (pejorative).

Blonde : *n.f.* – girlfriend.

Blouse : *n.f.* – woman's shirt, blouse.

Bobépine : *n.f.* – bobbypin.

Bobettes : *n.f.* – underwear, slip.

Boboche : *n.f.* – (badly-made) object or item.

Bœuf : *n.m.* – 1. *Fr.* Steer 2. *Fr.* pig, cop, police officer.

- *avoir un air de bœuf* – to be in a bad mood.
- *avoir un face de bœuf* – to be in a bad mood.

Boire : *v.t., v.t.* – *Fr.* to drink.

- *boire comme une éponge* – to drink like a sponge.
- *boire du fort* – to drink alcohol. *Lit.* to drink some strong [stuff]).
- *boire comme un biberon* – to drink like a fish. *Lit.* to drink like a baby's bottle.
- *boire comme un trou* – to drink like a fish. *Lit.* to drink like a hole.

Bois : *n.m.* – wood, woods.

- *bois franc* – hardwood.
- *bois mou* – soft wood.

sortir du bois – to make it out of the woods, to escape trouble.
Il a presque fini, mais il n'est pas encore sorti du bois. – He's almost done, but he's not out of the woods yet.

Boisé : *n.m.* – wooded area, glade.

Boisson : *n.f.* – *Fr.* drink.

de la boisson – (any) alcoholic drink.
être en boisson – to be drunk.

Boîte : *n.f.* – *Fr.* box.

boîte à malle – mailbox.
boîte à lunch – lunchbox.
Boîte vocale – voicemail.

Bolle : *n.f.* – intelligent person.

Bombe : *n.f.* – kettle.

Bompers : *n.m. pl.* – 1. bumpers (of a car, etc). 2. boobs, breasts.

(un) Bon : *adj.* – at least, a minimum (of something)

Ca va nous prendre un bon trois heures de route – It's going to take us a good three hours of driving to get there.

Bon Jack : *n.m.* – a good fellow, a forthright person.

(le) Bon vieux temps : *expr.* – *Fr.* the good old days.

Bonhomme Sept Heures : *n.m.* – the sandman.

Bonjour : *expr.* – Good Day. Used both as a greeting and a farewell.

Bonjour, là – See you, now!

Booker : *v.t.* – to schedule, to book.

Je vais booker une salle pour demain. – I'll book a room for tomorrow.

Booster : *v.t., v.t.* – 1. to provide moral support. 2. to jump-start a car.
J'ai besoin des câbles pour booster mon char. – I need cables so I can jump-start my car.

Bord : *n.m.* – side.

Sur le bord de la maison – On the other side of the house.
❧ *être sur l'autre bord* – to be pregnant.
❧ *passer sur l'autre bord* – to die.

Borné : *adj.* – pig-headed, stubborn.

Borne-fontaine : *n.f.* – firehydrant.

Bosse : *n.f.* – *Fr.* bump.

❧ *rouler sa bosse* – to show one's wisdom. *Lit.* "to roll one's bump".

Bosser : *v.t.* – to boss around, to play the head honcho. Used differently from French *bosser*, meaning "to work".

Lui, il n'arrête pas de bosser tout le monde. – He keeps pushing everybody around.

Botchage : *n.m.* – badly-done work.

Botcher : *v.t.* – to mess up, to botch, *sl.* to screw up.

Botte : *n.f.* – *Fr.* boot. 2. screw.

❧ *prendre une botte*★★★ – to screw, to have sex with.
❧ *(une) bonne botte*★★★ – a good screw, a good lay.
❧ *soule comme une botte* – completely wasted, inebriated. *Lit.* as drunk as a boot.

(se faire) Botter : *v.t. / v.i.* − to be kicked

 se faire botter le cul* − to get kicked in the ass.

Bottines : *n.f. pl.* − shoes, footwear.

Boucane : *n.f.* − smoke.

Boucaner : *v.t., v.i.* − to smoke.

Bouche : *n.f.* − *Fr.* mouth.

 avoir la bouche molle − to slur one's words (most notably, after drinking). *Lit.* 'to have a soft mouth.'

Boucher : *v.t.* − 1. *Fr.* to stop up, to close. 2. to shut up.

Il s'est fait boucher pas longtemps après. − He was forced to shut up not long afterwards.

Bouette : *n.f.* − mud, mire.

Bougonneux(euse) : *adj.* − grumpy.

Bouilli : *n.m.* − stew with meat and vegetables, similar to French *pot-au-feu*.

Bougrine : *n.f.* − overcoat, outerwear.

Boules** : *n.f. pl.* − *sl.* boobs, breasts.

Bouleversant(e) : *adj.* − staggering, bewildering, incredible.

On a eu des nouvelles bouleversantes ce soir. − We had staggering news this evening.

Bouleverser : *v.t.* − to shock, *sl.* to bowl over, *sl.* to blow away.

Les nouvelles m'ont pas mal bouleversé. − The news shook me quite a bit.

Bourrasser : *v.t.* – to be sharp, rude, bothersome.

Bourratif (–ive) : *adj.* – filling. (food)

Bourré : *adj.* – full (of food).

Bourse : *n.f.* – purse, handbag.

Bout(te) : *n.m.* 1. *Fr.* end, goal. 2. piece or part of something. 3. a while, a period of time.

- *au boutte* – 1. to the extreme. 2. to the end. 3. really good.
  Il l'a fait au boutte. – He did it right up to the end.
  Il est au boutte, ton char ! – Your car is the greatest!
  Je l'ai fait pour un boutte. – I did it for a while.
- *avoir le gros boutte du bâton* – to have the advantage *Lit.* to hold the big end of the stick).
- *faire un boutte* – to leave, to depart, to blow out of (somewhere).
- *sur le bout de la langue* – on the tip of (one's) tongue.
- *tenir le gros bout du bâton* – to have the advantage *Lit.* to hold the big end of the stick).

Boyau : *n.m.* – hose.

- *boyau d'arrosage* – watering hose.

Bozo–les–culottes : *n.m.* – clown, idiot. *Lit.* "the clown with the pants".

Brailler : *v.t.* – to cry.

Braillage : *n.m.* – crying, weeping.

Braker : *v.t.* – to brake, to slow down.

Brancher : *v.t.* − 1. *Fr.* to plug-in. 2. to decide, to make up (one's) mind.

Branchez-vous, les amis ! − Make up your minds, guys!

Branler : *v.t.* − to hesitate, take one's time.

⚜ *branler dans le manche* − to hesitate when making a decision. *Lit.* to hesitate in the handle.

Branleux(euse) : *n.m. / fem. & adj.* − one who is indecisive or hesitant.

Braoule : *n.f.* − large serving spoon.

Bras : *n.m.* − *Fr.* arm.

⚜ *coûter un bras* − to cost an arm (and a leg).
⚜ *huile à bras* − elbow-grease, real effort.
⚜ *sur le bras* − free, at no cost.

Brassière : *n.m.* − bra.

Break : *n.m.* − break.

⚜ *prendre un break* − 1. to take a break. 2. to stop dating someone temporarily (romantic sense).

Bretelles : *n.f. pl.* − suspenders, braces.

⚜ *(se) péter les bretelles* − to boast, to brag *Lit.* to snap one's suspenders.

Bretter : *v.t.* − 1. to dawdle, to waste time. 2. to drag on, to continue without end.

Arrête de bretter et viens donc avec moi ! − Stop wasting time and c'mon with me!

Breuvage : *n.m.* − beverage, drink.

Brisé(e) : *adj.* − 1. *Fr.* broken, out of order, malfunctioning. 2. depressed, down (for a person).

Broche : *n.f.* – 1. *Fr.* (steel-wire) staple. 2. (wire) pin.

    amanchure de broche à foin – badly organized mess. *Lit.* a haywire mess

    broche à foin – 1. a haywire (thing or person), something out of order. 2. bailing wire. *Lit.* hay staple.

Brocher : *v.t.* – *Fr.* to staple, attach.

Brocheuse : *n.f.* – *Fr.* stapler.

Brosse : *n.f.* – *Fr.* brush, hairbrush.

    prendre une brosse – to go on a bender, to get drunk.

    virer une brosse – to go on a bender, to get drunk.

Broue : *n.f.* – suds, foam.

    avoir de la broue dans le toupet – to have much work to do.

    faire de la broue – to blow hot air, to talk big.

Brûlement : *n.m.* – burning sensation.

(se) Brûler : *v.i.* – to burn one's self (out).

Je me suis vraiment brûlé pour livrer ca à temps – I really burned myself out to deliver that on time.

Brûlot : *n.m.* – mosquito.

Brun : *n.m.* – a Canadian $100 bill.

Brunante : *n.f.* – sunset, sundown.

Buanderie : *n.f.* – laundromat.

Bûche : *n.f.* – *Fr.* log.

    se tirer une bûche – to join in (a conversation, etc). *Lit.* to pull up a log.

Bûcher : *v.t.* – 1. to fell trees, to log. 2. to work hard.

Bucker : *v.t.* – to buck, to counter (something).

Bumper : *v.t.* – to move (something) out of the way, to bump.

   ❧ *se faire bumper* –, to be downgraded to be pushed out.

Bummer : *v.t., v.t.* – 1. to beg, bum (money). 2. to hang around.

Il avait du monde qui bummait du change dehors. – There were people bumming change outside.

Butin : *n.m.* – clothes.

Buzzant : *adj.* – impressive, amazing.

C

Ça : *pron.* – *Fr.* this, that.

- ❧ *Ça, là…* – And as for that…
- ❧ *Ça doit.* – That must be the case.
- ❧ *C'est ça qui est ça.* – Things will be as they are.
- ❧ *Ça fait que…* – so, therefore. *Lit.* "This makes it such that…"
- ❧ *Ça prend…* – That'll take… *Expr.* Very similar to French "*Il faut*", *Ca prend* is generally used to specify something necessary to identify a goal. Also used in the reflexive (*Ca me prends*, etc)

Ca prends deux minutes de ton temps – It'll take just 2 minutes of your time.

Ca va te prendre une cuillère pour le manger – You'll need a spoon to eat it.

Ca fait plaisir : *expr.* – "It's my pleasure"

Ca paraît : *expr.* – "That's clear."

Ça va (tu) bien? : *expr.* – 1. How are you doing? 2. Are you OK?

Cabane : *n.f.* – *Fr.* cabin, wood shack.

- ❧ *cabane à sucre* – sugar shack – a cabin in the woods once used in the production of maple syrup, and converted into a restaurant serving traditional Québec foodstuffs.

Cabaret : *n.m.* – tray.

Le serveur a rangé les assiettes sur son cabaret. – The waiter placed the plates on his tray.

Cachette : *n.f.* – hide-and-go-seek game.

- ❧ *jouer à la cachette* – to play hide-and-go-seek.

Cadran : *n.m.* – alarm clock.

Cailler : *v.i.* – to fall asleep.

Caler : *v.t.* – 1. to drink quickly, to swallow at a draught, *sl.* chug. 2. to drown.

Vas-y, cale ! – C'mon, drink up!

Câler : *v.t.* – to order, to call.

🦌 *câler (son) bluff* – to call (someone's) bluff.
🦌 *câler l'orignal* – to puke, to throw up. *Lit.* to call the moose.
On a déjà câlé trois pintes de bière. – We already ordered three pints of beer.

Câline★ : *expl.* – Dammit! (gentler form of *câlisse*).

Câlique★ : *expl.* – Dammit! (gentler form of *câlisse*).

Câlisse★★ : *expl.* – Goddamn! *Lit.* "chalice" from the Roman Catholic mass.

Câlisser★★ : *v.i., v.t.* – 1. to leave, to abandon. 2. to not care.

Je m'en câlisse★★ : I don't give a damn.
🦌 *câlisser (quelqu'un) dehors* – to throw (someone) out.
🦌 *câlisser une volée* – to beat (someone) up.

Câlissement★ : *adv.* – Goddam.

Calorifère : *n.m.* – *Fr.* electric heater (radiator).

Caltor★ : *expl.* – Dammit! (gentler form of *câlisse*.)

Calvaire★★ : *expl.* – Goddam *Lit.* "Calvary", where Christ was crucified).

Camion : *n.m.* – *Fr.* truck.

🦌 *camion de vidanges* – garbage truck.

Camionneur : *n.m.* − *Fr.* truck-driver, trucker.

Camisole : *n.f.* − woman's jumper, underwear.

Camp : *n.m.* − camp, camping place.

   sacrer son camp − to leave, to head out.

Canal : *n.m.* − channel, television station.

Canular : *n.m.* − candid camera.

Canceller : *v.t.* − to cancel, nullify.

Cancer : *n.m.* − old car, *sl.* rusted heap.

Cannages : *n.f. pl.* − canned products, conserves.

Cannone : *adj.* − striking, highly attractive (woman).

Canisse : *n.f.* − 1. milk drum. 2. can (of soda, beer, etc.).

Canter : *v.i.* − to fall asleep.

Cap de roue : *n.m.* − hubcap.

Capable (de) : *adj.* − 1. *Fr.* able, capable of (something). 2. to stand, to put up with.

   Lui, là, je suis pas capable. − I really can't stand that guy.

Capot : *n.m.* − winter coat.

   capot de poil − fur coat.

Capotant : *adj.* − unbelievable, phenomenal.

Capoté : *adj.* − crazy, out of control, *sl.* nuts.

Capoter : *v.t.* – to lose it, to go crazy, to get carried away.

Oui, j'ai vu ce film-là, ça m'a fait capoter ! – Yes, I saw that film – it made me completely lose it!

🌿 *capoter (bien) raide* – to panic, to lose one's head.

Carré : *n.m.* – park, square.

🌿 *Carré Saint-Louis* – Saint Louis Square.

Carreauté(e) : *adj.* – checked, checkered.

Il a mis un chandail carreauté. – He put on a checkered shirt.

Carrément : *adv. expr.* – *Fr.* frankly, honestly. *Lit.* squarely.

Je suis carrément crevé ! – Frankly, I'm bushed!

Carriole : *n.f.* – Carriage, cart.

🌿 *peau de carriole* – carriage blanket. Typically refers to blanket found in horse-drawn carriages. *Lit.* "cart skin".

Carrosse : *n.m.* – stroller, carriage.

Cartable : *n.m.* – binder, notebook.

Carte : *n.f.* – 1. *Fr.* card. 2. *Fr.* map.

🌿 *mettre (un endroit) sur la carte* – to put (someplace) on the map.

Carter : *v.i.* – to card (someone) to verify their age.

Carte-soleil : *n.f.* – Québec health insurance card.

Cas : *n.m.* – *Fr.* case, situation.

🌿 *en tout cas* – in any case, anyhow.

Cash : *n.m.* – 1. cash (money). 2. cash register.

S'il vous plaît, passez au cash après. – Please go to the checkout counter afterwards.

❦ *passer au cash* – to pay the price, to pay one's debt.

Casque : *n.m.* – *Fr.* helmet. Hat.

❦ *(en) avoir plein son casque* – to have enough. *Lit.* to have one's hat full.

❦ *casque de poil* – *n.m.* – fur hat.

❦ *casque de bain* – *n.m.* – showercap.

Cassé : *adj.* – 1. *Fr.* broken. 2. out of money, *sl.* broke.

❦ *cassé comme un clou* – completely broke. *Lit.* broke as a nail.

Casse-croûte : *n.m.* – Small snack restaurant, often found on the roadside in rural Québec.

Casse-tête : *n.m.* – puzzle. *Lit.* head breaker.

Casser : *v.i.* – 1. *Fr.* to break. 2. to break up, to split up.

Ils ont cassé il y a trois semaines environ. – They broke up about three weeks ago.

❦ *casser la croûte* – to grab a bite. *Lit.* to break a crust.

Casseux(euse) de party : *n.m.* – bore, *sl.* party-pooper.

Catalogne : *n.f.* – quilt.

Catcher : *v.t.* – to catch on, to get it, to understand.

J'ai pas tout catché. – I didn't get it all.

Catin : *n.m./f.* – 1. *Fr.* doll. 2. prostitute.

Caucus : *n.m.* – team discussion.

Cause : *n.f. – Fr.* reason, cause.

   🌼 *à cause que…* – because.

Cave : *adj., n.m. /f.* – moron, idiot (for an individual).

Cédule : *n.f.* – schedule, timeline.

Céduler : *v.t.* – to schedule, arrange a time for something.

CEGEP : *n.m.* – Québec junior college.

Cellulaire : *n.m.* – cellular phone.

Cenne : *n.f.* – cent, penny.

   J'ai plus une cenne ! – I don't have a cent left!

Centre d'achats : *n.m.* – mall, shopping center.

Certain : *adj.* – certainly, absolutely.

Cervelle : *n.f. – Fr.* brain, head, *sl.* noggin.

   Je ne sais pas comment faire rentrer cette idée dans sa cervelle. – I don't know how to get that idea into his noggin.
   🌼 *avoir mal à la cervelle* – to have a headache.

Certain : *adv.* – certainly, definitely.

   🌼 *Ca fonctionne, certain.* – That definitely works.

C'est en plein ça : *expr.* – That's exactly it.

Chaise berçante : *n.f.* – rocking chair.

Chambalant(e) : *adj.* – rickety, unstable.

Chambre de bain : *n.f.* – bathroom.

Champ : *n.m. — Fr.* field.

    ☘ *être dans le champ* — to be in error, to be mistaken. *Lit.* to be in the field.

Champlure : *n.m. —* faucet, tap.

Chance : *n.f. — Fr.* luck

    ☘ *prendre une chance* — to take a chance.

Chanceux(euse) : *n.m. /fem. & adj. — Fr.* one who is lucky.

Chandail : *n.m. —* long-sleeve shirt, sweater.

Change : *n.m. —* coinage, loose change, spare change.

    ☘ *prendre tout son petit change* — to take a tremendous effort. *Lit.* to take all one's spare change.

Changer : *v.t., v.i. — Fr.* to change.

    ☘ *changer d'idée* — 1. to change (one's) mind. 2. to take a break.
    ☘ *changer d'air* — to change one's mood or state of mind. *Il doit changer d'air s'il veut s'amuser ce soir.* — He needs to change his state of mind if he wants to have fun tonight.
    ☘ *changer quatre trente sous pour une piastre* — 1. to make no profit. 2. to change one thing for another of identical value. *Lit.* to change thirty cents for a quarter.

Chansonnier : *n.m. —* singer/song-writer.

Chanter : *v.t., v.i. — Fr.* to sing

    ☘ *chanter la pomme* — to flirt. *Lit.* to sing the apple.

Chapeau : *n.m. — Fr.* hat.

    ☘ *parler à travers son chapeau* — to blow hot air, to speak without actual knowledge. *Lit.* "to speak across one's hat".

Char : *n.m.* – automobile, truck.

- *avoir son char* – to be fed up.
- *avoir vu passer des gros chars* – to have experience. *Lit.* "to have seen big cars go by".
- *char de marde*★★ – deep shit. *Lit.* "a car of shit".
  Je suis vraiment dans un char de marde avec ma blonde – I'm in seriously deep shit with my girlfriend.
- *char de police* – police car.

Charger : *v.t.* – to charge, to bill.

Combien tu charges pour celui-là ? – How much do you charge for this one?

Charge renversée : *expr.* – collect (telephone call).

Châroéyer : *v.t.* – (professional) transporter.

Charrue : *n.f.* – snowplow.

Châssis : *n.m.* – 1. window. 2. window pane.

Chat : *n.f.* – *Fr.* cat.

- *Il n'y a pas un chat.* – There's no one (there).
- *chat sauvage* – raccoon.

Chaud : *adj.* – 1. *Fr.* hot, warm. 2. tipsy, slightly drunk.

Chaudasse : *adj.* – tipsy, slightly drunk.

Chaudière : *n.f.* – 1. bucket, metal pail. 2. lunchbox.

Chaudron : *n.m* – cookpot.

Chauffer : *v.t., v.i.* – 1. *Fr.* to warm. 2. to drive.

Tasse-toué, je veux chauffer un peu. – Move over, I want to drive for a bit.

❧ *chauffer les fesses* – to give a spanking. *Lit.* to warm the buttocks.

Chauffrette : *n.f.* – portable (electric) heater.

Chaumière : *n.f.* – *Fr.* cottage, country house.

Chausson au Pommes : *n.m* – *Fr.* Apple pastry

❧ *Et un chausson avec ça ?* – *equiv.* "Would you like fries with that?"

Chaussettes : *n.f. pl.* – slippers.

Checker : *v.t.* – 1. to verify. 2. to keep an eye on, to guard. 3. to check out, to look at.

❧ *Je vais checker voir.* – I'll check and see.
❧ *Peux-tu checker mes bagages pour deux secondes ?* – Can you keep an eye on my bags for a few seconds?
❧ *Checke la fille là-bas !* – Check out that girl over there!

Chemin : *n.m.* – *Fr.* path, road, way.

❧ *chemin de garnotte* – gravel road.
❧ *chemin de gravelle* – gravel road.

Chèque de voyage : *n.f* – traveller's check.

Chevreuil : *n.m.* – deer, buck.

Chez : *prep.* – at the home of (someone). Québécers almost always use the plural form (chez nous, chez vous, chez eux), even when speaking about a residence with only one person

J'm'en va chez nous. – I'm going back to my place.

Chiâleux(euse) : *adj. & n.m./fem.* – grumpy, crabby, ill – tempered.

Chiâler : *v.i.* – to complain, *sl.* to bitch. *N.B.* In France this word implies crying or weeping, not complaining.

Chiard : *n.m.* – 1. beef stew. 2. difficulty, complex issue.

    être dans un beau chiard – to be in trouble. *Lit.* to be in a nice stew.

Chicane : *n.f.* – argument, dispute.

    chicane de ménage – household argument.
    pogner une chicane – to have an argument.

Chicoter : *v.i.* – to bother, to disturb.

    Ça m'a chicoté toute la nuit. – It bothered me all night long.

Chien : *adj.* – 1. *Fr.(n.)* dog. 2. chicken, fraidy-cat. 3. mean (person)

    Il pourrait, mais il est trop chien pour le faire – He could, but he's too afraid to do it.
    avoir du chien – to have determination or character. *Lit.* to have some dog.
    son chien est mort (expr)– to be done-in, to be finished. *Lit.* his dog is dead.

Chiendent : *n.m.* – weeds, dog's-tooth grass.

    avoir du chiendent – to have a lot of character.

Chienne** : *n.f.* – *Fr.* bitch. *Lit.* female dog. A derogatory term for a girl.

    avoir la chienne – to be afraid, to be worried.
    avoir l'air de la chienne à Jacques – to be badly dressed. *Lit.* to seem like Jacques' dog.

Chier★★★ : *v.t., v.i. − Fr.* to shit.

- ❧ *Va chier !* − Piss off!
- ❧ *Va chier un lunch au large !*★★ − Go take a fuckin' hike!
- ❧ *chier de l'or en barre*★ − to believe oneself to be special. *Lit.* to shit bars of gold.
- ❧ *chier dans (ses) culottes*★★ − to be afraid, to shit in (one's) pants.
- ❧ *Faire chier* − to suck, to be bad.
  Ça fait chier ! − That sucks!

Chieux : *adj. & n.m. /fem.* − scared, coward.

Chigner : *v.i.* − to whine, to snivel.

Chiottes★★ : *n.f. pl.* − toilet, bathroom. *Lit.* "the shitters"

Chnolles★★ : *n.f. pl.* − balls, testicles.

Chnoute★★ : *n.f.* − shit.

Cette affaire-là, c'est juste de la chnoute. − That thing is a total piece of shit.

Choqué(e) : *adj.* − angry, perturbed.

(se) Choquer : *v.i.* − to become angry.

Chose bine : *pron.* − what's-his-name.

Je parlais avec chose bine, là… − I was talking with what's-his-name…

Chotte : *n.f.* − shot.

- ❧ *boire d'une chotte* − to gulp down.
- ❧ *(faire quelquechose)… d'une (seule) chotte* − (to do something) all at once, (do something) in a single shot.

Chou : *n.m.* − 1. cabbage. 2. Darling (term of endearment)

Chouclaques : *n.m.* – sneakers, running shoes.

Chromo★★ : *n.m.* – troll, ugly person.

Chum : *n.m.* – 1. boyfriend (female referring to male). 2. friend (male referring to male).

🌿 *être ben chum avec (quelqu'un)* – to be really chummy with (someone)

Chu : *pron.* – *Contr.* Je.

Ciarge : *n.f.* – slang, patois.

Ciboire : *expl.* – Goddamit!

Cigne : *n.m.* – kitchen sink.

Cimonaque : *expl.* – Dammit!

Cinquante-sous : *n.m* – fifty-cent piece.

Circulaire : *n.f.* – advertisements, junk mail.

Je reçois constamment des circulaires sous ma porte. – I'm constantly getting advertisements under my door.

Citron : *adj., n.m.* – *Fr.* lemon. Often used as a pejorative word for a car.

🌿 *se faire passer un citron* – to be handed a lemon.

Clair(e) : *adj.* – clear, lucid.

Clairer : *v.t.* – to clear up, finish, clear out.

On va clairer de l'espace pour les nouveaux meubles. – We'll make some space for the new furniture.
🌿 *se faire clairer* – to be thrown out (of a bar, etc.).

Clancher : *v.i.* – 1. to accelerate violently. 2. to work well, *sl.* to take off.

> *Oui, notre business commence à clancher.* – Our business is really starting to take off.

Claque : *n.f.* – *Fr.* slap.

> ❦ *donner la claque* – to give it your best.

Claques : *n.f. pl.* – rubbers, boots.

Clavarder : *v.i.* – to chat on the Internet. *Contr.* "*clavier*" and "*bavarder*".

Clenche : *n.f.* – latch (of a door, etc.).

Clôture : *n.f.* – *Fr.* gate.

> ❦ *sauter la clôture* – to cheat on one's spouse. *Lit.* "to jump the gate".

Cliquer : *v.i.* – 1. to make sense, *sl.* to click (an idea). 2. to work well.

> *Je lui ai expliqué cinq fois, mais il n'a pas encore cliqué.* – I've explained it to him five times, but it still hasn't clicked.
> *Ça clique!* – That works!

Clou : *n.m.* – *Fr.* nail.

> ❦ *cassé comme un clou* – *sl.* broke, penniless. *Lit.* broke as a nail.
> ❦ *cogner des clous* – to be nodding off (to sleep). *Lit.* to drive nails in.
> ❦ *tomber comme des clous* – to rain heavily. *Lit.* to fall like nails.

Coche : *n.f.* – groove, cut, notch.

> ❦ *monter d'une coche* – to go up a notch.

Cochon : *n.m.* – *Fr.* pig.

  prendre la passe du cochon qui tousse – to cut corners, to take a
  shortcut. *Lit.* "to take the way of the coughing pig".

Cochon(ne) : *adj. & n.m./fem.* – dirty (in a sexual sense). *Lit.* pig-
like.

Cocotte : *n.f.* – pine cone.

Code régional : *n.m.* – area code (telephone).

Cœur : *n.m.* – *Fr.* heart.

  avoir une crotte sur le cœur – to have a chip on one's shoulder, to
  be prejudiced against someone.

Coin : *n.m.* – *Fr.* corner.

  tourner les coins ronds – to steer clear of problems. *Lit.* to turn
  rounded corners.

Coincé : *adj. & n.m. fem.* – 1. narrow-minded (person) 2. stuck,
backed into a corner (literally or figuratively).

  Ce gars-là, je l'ai toujours trouvé un peu coincé. – I've always found
  that guy to be kind've narrow-minded.

Col-bleu : *n.m.* – blue-collar (worker).

Collant : *adj.* – clingy, hanger-on (for a person).

Colle : *n.f.* – *Fr.* glue

  ne pas valoir de la colle – to be worthless, to be of bad quality.
  Lit. "to not be worth glue".

(se) Coller : *v.t., v.i.* − 1. *Fr.* to stick, to glue. 2. to curl up with, to snuggle against.

    coller comme la misère sur le pauvre monde − to be firmly attached to (something). *Lit.* to stick as misery to the poor.

Colleux : *n.m.* − 1. hug. 2. clingy person.

Coloc : *n.m. /fem.* − roommate, joint tenant. *Contr.* colocataire.

Colon : *n.m. & adj.* − 1. idiot, moron. 2. bumpkin, redneck. 3. tasteless, gaudy.

Combines : *n.f. pl.* − long-johns, full-length underwear.

Combler : *v.t.* − to fill, to provide.

Commande : *n.f.* − order.

    faire la commande − to go (food) shopping.

Comment : *adv.* − 1. *Fr.* how. 2. how much.

    Comment ça va faire ? − How much will that be?

Comme : *conj.* − *Fr.* as.

    comme du monde − as everyone else (is). *Lit.* "as other folks"
    comme quoi que − given that.

Compagnie : *n.f.* − company.

Compléter : *v.t.* − *Fr.* to fill out, complete.

    S'il vous plaît, compléter le formulaire − Please fill out the form.

Compote : *n.m.* − *Fr.* 1. Compost (bin) 2. fruit jam

    tomber en compote − to fall to pieces. *Lit.* "fall into fruit jam"

Comprenable : *adj.* − comprehensible, understan-dable.

Comptable agréé : *n.m* – chartered accountant.

Comptant : *adj.* – *Fr.* cash.

❧ *payer comptant* – to pay in cash.

Comptoir : *n.m.* – counter.

Je l'ai mis sur le comptoir. – I put it on the counter.

Comté : *n.m.* – county.

Concerné : *adj.* – involved, concerned.

❧ *en autant que je sois concerné* – as far as I'm concerned.

Concerner : *v.i.* – to be involved, to be concerned with (something).

En autant que ça me concerne… – Insofar as it involves me…

Confortable : *adj.* – comfortable, at ease.

Congédier : *v.t.* – to fire, to let go of an employee. *Lit.* to vacation.

Conjoint : *n.m.* – life partner.

Connecter : *v.t.* – to connect, plug together.

Conservateur : *n.m. /fem. & adj.* – moderate, conser-vative.

(se) Contrecâlisser★★ : *v.i.* – to not give a shit, to not care, to ignore.

Je m'en contrecâlisse s'il vient ou pas. – I don't give a shit if he comes along or not.

(se) Contrecrisser★★ : *v.i.* – to not give a shit, to not care, to ignore.

Je m'en contrecrisse s'il vient ou pas. – I don't give a shit if he comes along or not.

Contrôler : *v.t.* – to control. *N.B.* Different from International French, in which it means "to verify or insure".

Contrôle : *n.m.* – *Fr.* control.

☙ *sous contrôle* – under control.

Coquelœil- *adj.* – blind as a bat.

Coquerelle : *n.f.* – cockroach.

Coqueron : *n.m.* – tiny apartment, *sl.* a closet.

Corde à linge : *n.f.* – washline, clothesline.

☙ *passer la nuit sur la corde à linge* – to sleep badly. *Lit.* "to sleep on the clothesline".

Corps : *n.m.* – *Fr.* body.

☙ *veillée au corps* – a funeral wake (ceremony).

Correct : *adj.* – okay, successful, in order, correct, acceptable.

☙ *C'est-tu correct?* – Is it ok?

Correspondre : *v.i.* – to contact, to correspond (with someone).

Cossin : *n.m.* – small thing, object.

Costaud : *adj.* – stocky, well-built, strong (for a person).

Peut-être qu'il est petit, mais il est costaud! – He might be small, but he's built!

Costume de bain : *n.m.* – bathing suit.

Cotation : *n.f.* – quotation, statement of price.

Côtes levées : *n.f. pl.* – spareribs.

Côté : *n.m.* – side

☙ *être sur l'autre coté* – to be pregnant.
☙ *passer sur l'autre coté* – to die.

Coton : *n.m. – Fr.* cotton.

> *être au coton* – 1. to be at the end of one's means or patience. 2. to be exhausted.
> *faire coton* – to be pathetic.

(se) Coucher : *v.t. – Fr.* to go to bed.

> *se coucher les fesses à l'air* – to sleep butt-naked. *Lit.* to sleep with one's cheeks to the wind.

Coude : *n.m. – Fr.* elbow.

> *Se lever le coude* – to have several beers. *Lit.* to lift one's elbow.

Coudon : *expr. –* C'mon! *Def.* Ecoute, donc.

Couenne : *n.f. –* skin.

> *avoir la couenne dure* – to be thick-skinned.

Coulante : *adj. –* slippery (surface, etc).

Couler : *v.i. –* 1. *Fr.* to run, to drip (for a liquid). 2. to blow it, to fail.

Je crois qu'il va encore couler son affaire. – I think he's going to blow it again.

> *couler (quelque chose) dans le béton* – to cast (something) in stone.

Coulisse : *n.f. –* drippings.

Coup : *n.m. –* 1. *Fr.* a drink. 2. a blow.

> *avoir un coup dans le nez* – to have drunk a lot.
> *boire un coup* – to grab a drink.
>   *Il a reçu deux coups à la tête.* – He took two blows to the head.
> *coup de fil* – phone call.
> *lâcher un coup de fil* – to give someone a phone call.

Couper : *v.t.* – *Fr.* to cut, to reduce.

  ❧ *couper le prix* – to cut the price.

Cour à scrap : *n.m.* – junkyard.

Courâiller : *v.i.* – 1. to chase skirts, to womanize. 2. to run errands.

Courâilleux : *n.m.* – skirt-chaser, womanizer.

Coureux (-euse) : *n.m./f & adj* – one who likes to travel.

  ❧ *gang de coureux* – group that enjoyes travel together.

Courir : *v.i.* – *Fr.* to run.

  ❧ *courir la galipote* – to galivant, to chase women.

Courriel : *n.m.* – electronic mail (email).

Coutellerie : *n.f.* – cutlery, utentils.

Coûter : *v.i.* – *Fr.* to cost.

  ❧ *coûter un bras* – to cost an arm (and a leg).

  ❧ *couter la peau des fesses* – to cost a fortune. *Lit.* "to cost the skin off your butt".

  ❧ *coûter les yeux de la tete* – to cost a fortune. *Lit.* "to cost the eyes in your head".

Couvert : *n.m.* – cover, lid.

Couverte : *n.f.* – blanket, cover.

Crampant : *adj.* – funny, hilarious. *Lit.* causing cramps.

Cramper : *v.i.* – to laugh to the point of doubling over. *Equiv.* "to laugh to the point of tears"

Crampé(e) : *adj.* – highly amused. *Lit.* bent in two.

J'étais crampé à cause de ce qu'il a dit. – I was doubled over by what he said.

Crapaud : *adj.* – wily, crafty, untrustworthy.

En affaires, il est crapaud. – In terms of business, he's not very trustworthy.

Crayon : *n.m.* – pen, pencil.

avoir de la mine dans le crayon★ – to have a ravenous sexual appetite. *Lit.* to have lead in the pencil.

Cré : *adj.* – "Good old". Used to refer affectionately or ironically to a person, and/or their traits.

Cré Jean, il est venu nous aider ènéouai ! – Good ol' Jean, he came to help us anyway!

Crèche : *n.f.* – orphanage. Whereas *crèche* means "daycare" in France, Québécois generally use *garderie* instead.

Crémage : *n.m.* – icing.

Crère : *v.t., v.i.* – believe. *Def. croire.*

Crée-moi, je suis sincère – Believe me, i'm not kidding.
Tu dois me crère ! – You gotta believe me!

Crémage : *n.m.* – icing.

Crème à barbe : *n.f.* – shaving cream.

Crème glacée : *n.f.* – ice cream.

Crémone : *n.f.* – long, knit scarf.

Cretons : *n.m. pl.* − *pâté* made from veal or pork, usually eaten at breakfast.

Creux : *adj.* − 1. *Fr.* deep. 2. far away, isolated.

Crever : *v.i.* − *Fr.* 1. to burst or deflate 2. to die, to fail

❧ *crever le ballon de quelqu'un* − to burst someone's bubble.

Crevant(e) : *adj* − hilarious, really funny

C'est un gars crevant − He's a really funny guy.

Criard : *n.m.* − car horn.

Crime! : *expr.* − Heck!

Crin : *n.m.* − *Fr.* horse-hair.

❧ *avoir les oreilles dans le crin* − 1. to be careful, fearing something or someone. 2. to be in a bad mood. *Lit.* to have one's ears in horse-hair.

Crinqué : *adj. & n.m/f.* − pissed off, angry (person).

Crinquer : *v.t.* − to crank, to wind (up). Used both in the figurative ("to crank someone up") and literal ("to crank a winch") senses.

Il l'a rendu complement crinqué sur l'idee de prendre sa poste lors de son départ. − He got her totally wound up about taking over his position when he leaves.

Crise : *n.f.* − 1. *Fr.* crisis. 2. fit.

❧ *piquer une crise* − to throw a fit. Different from International French in which this means "to faint".

Crisse★★ : *Expl.* − Goddamit. *Lit.* Christ.

❧ *Ben, crisse!* − Oh, hell…
❧ *Petit crisse* − traitor, two-faced person.

Crissant★ : *adj.* – a pain in the ass.

Crissement★ : *adv.* – (one hell of) a lot

Crisser★ : *v.i.* – 1. to leave. 2. *se crisser de (quelque chose)* – to not give a damn about (something).

- *crisser dehors* – to throw (someone/something) out.
- *crisser son camp* – to leave, *sl.* to blow out of somewhere
- *crisser un volée* – to teach someone a lesson (with physical force)
  S'il n'arret pas de me faire chier, je vais lui crisser un volée bientôt !★ – If he doesn't stop pissing me off, i'm going to teach his ass a lesson pretty soon!

Croche : *adj.* – *Fr.* bad, nasty, dishonest.

- *avoir des idées croches* – to have bad (dishonest) thoughts.
- *avoir les yeux (tout) croches* – to have squinty eyes.
- *être tout croche* – 1. to be bad. 2. to be dirty, distasteful. 3. to be hung over.
- *penser croche* – to think dirty (in a sexual sense).
- *se sentir (tout) croche* – to feel (really) bad, to be unhappy.

(se) Crosser★★★ : *v.i.* – 1. to wank, to masturbate. 2. to counter, to go against.

- *se faire crosser* – to be screwed over, to be betrayed.
  Je ne veux pas me faire crosser là-dessus. – I don't want to be screwed over on this.

Crosseur(euse)★ : *n.m./fem.* – cheat, traitor, hypocrit.

Cru : *adj.* – *Fr.* raw. Often used to describe the weather (raw & cold).

Cruiser : *v.t.* − 1. to hit on (someone), to make a pass at (someone). 2. to go out cruising.

> *Il n'a pas arrêté de la cruiser toute la soirée.* − He didn't stop hitting on her all night.

Cruising-bar : *expr.* − meat-market, pick-up joint.

Cul : *n.m.* − 1. *Fr.* end. 2. *Fr.* ass★★.

- *avoir le bec en cul de poule*★ − to have a continental French accent. Typically refers to someone who retains a French accent, despite several generations of family history in Québec Province. *Lit.* "to have one's face in a hen's bottom".
- *avoir juste le cul et les dents* − 1. to have no personality. 2. to be extremely thin. *Lit.* "to have just ass and teeth".
- *avoir le trou de cul en dessous du bras*★★ − to be exhausted. *Lit.* to have one's asshole under the arm.
- *se faire botter le cul*★ − to get kicked in the ass.

Culottes : *n.f.* − pants.

- *les culottes à terre* − with (one's) pants down.

D

D'abord : *adv.* – 1. *Fr.* first. 2. already.

Je vais tinker mon char d'abord. – I'm going to fill up my car first.
Dis-moi, d'abord ! – Tell me, already!

❧ *OK d'abord !* – OK then, that's fine.
❧ *d'abord que* – since, given that.
D'abord que tu y vas, moi j'ai pas besoin. – Since you're going, I don't need to.

Dactylo : *n.m.* – typewriter.

Danse : *n.f.* – *Fr.* dance.

❧ *Danse carrée* – square dance.

Dash : *n.m.* – dashboard (of a car).

❧ *fesser dans le dash-* to be surprising, to be unexpected.

Date : *n.m.* – *Fr.* date (day). Date, romantic meeting.

❧ *à date* – until now, up to this point.

de même : *adv.* – like this/that.

Je n'aime pas les gars de même. – I don't like guys like that.

de plus : *expr.* – Additionally, Also.

de quoi : *pron.* – something.

Je voudrais bien faire de quoi. – I'd really like to do something.

de suite : *expr.* – right away, immediately.

On va faire ça de suite – We'll do that right away.

Débâcle : *n.m.* – *Fr.* debacle, messy situation.

❧ *avoir le débâcle* – to have the runs, to have diarrhea.

Débalancé : *adj.* – out of whack, unbalanced.

Débalancer : *v.t.* – to throw out of whack, to unbalance.

Débarbouillette : *n.f.* – washcloth.

Débarque : *n.f.* – fall.

❧ *prendre une débarque* – to take a fall.

Débarquer : *v.t., v.i.* – 1. to take down. 2. to exit from a vehicle. 3. to quit.

On est débarqué de son char juste à côté de la piste. – We got out of the car right next to the ski slope.
Tout de même, Jacques va débarquer du conseil d'administration l'année prochaine. – Even so, Jacques will leave the board of directors next year.

Débarrer : *v.t.* – to unlock.

Je viens de débarrer la porte. – I just unlocked the door.

Débâtir : *v.t.* – to demolish, to knock down. *Lit.* to unbuild.

Ils vont débâtir la vieille église demain. – They're going to demolish the old church tomorrow.

(se) Débeurrer : *v.t. /v.i.* – to clean up, to wash up. Typically used only for a person, in a literal sense.

Débile : *adj. & n.m.* – awesome, unbelievable, insane. Can be used in a positive or negative sense.

C'est débile, ce film-là ! – That film is just amazing!

Débiné : *adj.* – depressed, demotivated.

Débiner : *v.i.* − to depress, to demotivate.

Sa copine l'a quitté, alors il est mal débiné − His girlfriend left him, so he's pretty depressed.

Décâlissant★ : *adj.* − depressing, a downer.

Décâlissé★ : *adj.* − 1. depressed, down, heartbroken. (Used for a person). 2. Damaged, destroyed. (Used for an object)

Décâlisser★ : *v.t.* − 1. to depart. 2. to depress.

Décapant : *n.m.* − Coca-Cola.

Déconcrissé : *adj.* − in pieces, in ruins.

Déconcrisser : *v.t.* − to demolish, to destroy.

Décrissant★ : *adv.* − depressing, a downer.

Décrissé★ : *adj.* − bummed out, disappointed, let down.

Moi, j'étais vraiment décrissé après. − I was really bummed out afterwards.

Décrisser★ : *v.i.* − 1. to beat it, to leave, to depart. 2. to damage, to ruin.

 Hé! décrisse de là! − Hey you! get the heck outa here!

Décrivable : *adj.* − describable, able to be explained.

Ma situation n'est pas vraiment décrivable. − I can't really describe my situation.

Décrocher : *v.t., v.i.* − 1. Fr. to stall, to lose momentum. 2. to fail, give up.

Lui, il décroche encore de l'école. − He's failing in school again.

Décrocheur (-euse) : *n.m/f.* − (school) drop-out.

Dedans : *prep.* − in, within.

🌿 *en dedans que…* − in less than…

Défaite : *n.m.* − excuse, pretense.

J'ai un défaite pour avoir manquer son partie. − I have an excuse for missing his party.

Dégêné : *adj.* − relaxed, at ease.

(se) Dégêner : *v.t.* − to loosen up, to relax.

Définitivement : *adv.* − definitely, certainly.

(se) Dégréyer : *v.i.* − 1. to take one's coat off, to get undressed. 2. to clear a table after a meal.

Va te dégréyer et reste donc un peu. − Take your coat off and stay a while, then!
Veux-tu me dégrayer la table, s'il te plaît ? − Would you clear the table for me, please ?

Dégrincher : *v.t.* − to destroy, to undo.

(se) Dégripper : *v.t.* − to get better, to heal up.

(se) Déguédiner : *v.i.* − to hurry up, to move quickly.

Déjeuner : *v.i.* − to have breakfast.

Déjeuner : *n.m.* − breakfast. In France *petit-déjeuner* usually implies breakfast, and *déjeuner* implies lunch.

Démancher : *v.t.* − to take off, remove, take down.

(à) Demure : *adj.* − 1. Well-built, well-contructed. 2. Completely, totally

Demeurer : *v.i.* – to live, to reside in.

On demeure à Montréal en ce moment. – We live in Montreal at the moment.

(se) Déniaiser : *v.i.* – to wise up, to smarten up.

Dep : *contr.* – Dépanneur (convenience store).

   passer au dép. – swing by the convenience store.

Dépanneur : *n.m.* – 1. convenience store. 2. *Fr.* towing company.

Dépareillé(e) : *adj.* – unique, remarkable.

Dépasser : *v.t.* – 1. *Fr.* to pass. 2. to pass (in a car).

Il n'arrête jamais de dépasser des autos sur l'autoroute. – He never stops passing other cars on the highway.

Dépendamment : *adv.* – depending on, as a function of (something).

Dépeinturer : *v.t.* – to strip, to remove the paint from (something).

Il faut d'abord que je dépeinture le mur. – I have to strip the wall first.

Dépense : *n.f.* – 1. cupboard, cabinet. 2. *Fr.* cost, expenditure.

   au diable la dépense – to hell with the price. *Lit.* to the devil with the price.

Dépensier(e) : *n.m./fem.* – spendthrift.

Dérangeant(e) : *adj.* – disturbing, bothersome.

Déraincher : *v.t.* – to destroy, to undo.

Dérencher : *v.t.* – to pull (out), to dislocate.

Ca c'est la troisième fois qu'il s'est dérenché le coudre. – This is the third time he'd dislocated his elbow.

Dérougir : *v.i.* – to reduce, to diminish, to cease.

(se) Désâmer : *v.i.* – to work oneself to the bone, to give (something) one's all (in a job, or other task). *Lit.* "to de-soul oneself".

Ca fait quatre ans qu'il se désâme chez eux, sans aucun mot pour lui rémercier – He's worked himself to the bone for four years there, without so much as a 'thank you'.

Descendre : *v.i, v.t.* – *Fr.* to descend, to go down.

🌿 *descendre tous les saints du ciel* – to swear. *Lit.* to bring down all the saints from the heavens.

Désennui : *n.m.* – pastime, diversion, hobby.

Deshe★★★ : *n.f.* – sperm, semen.

Désouffler : *v.t.* – to let the air out (of something).

Détail : *n.m.* – *Fr.* detail, particular.

🌿 *à cheval sur les détails* – hung up on the details. *Lit.* on horseback about the details.

Déteindu(e) : *adj.* – faded, discolored. *Lit.* un-tinted.

Dévirer : *v.i.* – to turn aside, to change direction.

Diable : *n.m.* – *Fr.* devil.

🌿 *Le diable est aux vaches* – Used to describe a chaotic situation. *Lit.* "the devil is with the cows".

🌿 *mener le diable* – to make a racket, cause a disturbance.

🌿 *tirer le diable par la queue* – to be very poor. *Lit.* to pull the devil by the tail.

D'ici : *conj.* – From now until…

D'ici un an – within a year.

Différencer : *v.t.* – to distinguish, to tell the difference between (things).

Moi, je ne peux pas différencer les deux. – I can't tell the two apart.

(faire du) Diguidi ha ha : *v.i.* – 1. to screw around (joking sense). 2. To screw around (sexual sense)

Dîner : *n.m.* – lunch.

Dire : *v.t.* – *Fr.* to say.

🌿 *avoir pour son dire que…* – to think that… *Lit.* 'to have for his say (that)…'

(C'est pas) Disable : *expr.* – incredible, indescribable. *Lit.* "sayable"

Dîner : *v.i.* – to have lunch.

Disconnecter : *v.t.* – to disconnect, unplug.

Discontinuer : *v.t.* – to discontinue, stop producing.

Dispendieux(euse) : *adj.* – *Fr.* costly, expensive.

Dix cennes : *n.m.* – penny, 10-cent piece.

Dix-huit roues : *n.m.* – 18-wheeler (truck).

Dodicher : *v.t.* – to cradle an infant (in one's arms).

Dompe : *n.f.* – dump, waste disposal site.

Domper : *v.t.* – to throw out, to dump.

Donner : *v.t., v.i.* − 1. *Fr.* to give. 2. to seem, to appear (when speaking about the result of something).

> *Ça donne le bon effet.* − That yields the right effect.
> *Ça donne un peu trop compliqué.* − That seems a bit complicated.
> ❧ *donner la bascule* − traditional Québec birthday practice of grabbing someone by shoulders and ankles and tossing them into the air the same number of times as their age. *Lit.* to give someone the seesaw.
> ❧ *donner un bec sur la suce* − to give someone a kiss on the lips.
> ❧ *donner la claque* − to give it your best.
> ❧ *donner le diable à (quelqu'un)* − to give (someone) hell.
> ❧ *donner un lift* − to give (someone) a lift.
> ❧ *donner de la merde à (quelqu'un)** − to give (someone) shit.
> ❧ *donner de la misère à (quelqu'un)* − to give (someone) a hard time.
> ❧ *donner du slack à (quelqu'un)*− to give (someone) some slack.
> ❧ *donner son 4%* − to send away, to fire. A reference to the standard four percent vacation pay in Québec, typically reimbursed upon termination of employment.
> ❧ *Donnes-y la claque !* − Give it a try!

Dorénavant : *adv.* − *Fr.* henceforth, from this time on.

Dormir : *v.i.* − *Fr.* to sleep.

> ❧ *dormir sur la switch* − to waste time, to be slow. *Lit.* to sleep on the switch.
> ❧ *dormir au gaz* − to waste time, to be slow. *Lit.* to sleep on the gas.

Dos : *n.m.* − *Fr.* back, rear-side.

> ❧ *parler dans le dos de quelqu'un* − to talk behind someone's back.

Douance : *n.f.* − intelligence, qualities of a gifted person.

Doudou : *n.f.* − blanket, comforter.

Douillette : *n.f.* – blanket, comforter.

Doux : *adj.* – *Fr.* soft

    doux comme un agneau – very polite, very gentle. Usually said of someone kind.

Down : *n.m.* – period of depression or malcontent.

Après que mon chum m'a quittée, j'ai eu un gros down. – After my boyfriend left me, I was really down for a while.

Down : *adj.* – down, depressed.

Drap : *n.m.* – *Fr.* sheet, curtain.

    être blanc comme un drap – to be as white as a sheet.

(à) Drette : *n.m.* – *1. (to the) right. Def. (à) droite. 2. straight.*

    drette là – *right there.*
    tout drette – *straight ahead.*
    Drette à soir… – As of this evening…

Driver : *v.t.* – to be in charge of, to be in control of, to drive.

C'est toi qui vas driver ce projet? – You're the one who will drive this project?

Drôle : *adj.* – 1. *Fr.* funny, amusing 2. funny (strange, weird)

    (une) drôle d'affaire – strange situation.

Dropper : *v.t.* – 1. to drop, to let go (of something). 2. to plummet downwards.

Je vais le dropper, s'il continue de même. – I'll let him go if he continues like this.

Dû : *adj.* – due, required.

  ❧ *dû à...* – due to...
  ❧ *dû pour...* – due for...
    Mon char est dû pour un changement d'huile. – My car is due for an oil change.

Dull : *adj.* – boring, dull.

  ❧ *dull à mourir* – deathly boring.

Dumper : *v.t.* – 1. to throw away 2. to drop (someone) off. 3. to break up with (someone)

    Ma blonde m'a dumpé il y a trois jours. – My girlfriend dumped me three days ago.

Dur : *adj.* – 1. *Fr.* hard. 2. difficult.

  ❧ *faire dur* – 1. to be in a bad situation or state, to be rough. 2. To be idiotic, ridiculous, ugly, or crazy. 3. To be badly dressed.
    Ça fait un peu dur. – That's kind of a difficult situation.

Durant que : *conj.* – while, during.

E

É : *Expr.* – She is. *Def.* "*Elle est*".

Eau : *n.f.* – *Fr.* water.

> *avoir de l'eau dans la cave* – to wear pants that are too short. *Lit.* "to have water in the cave".
> *être dans l'eau bouillante (chaud)* – to be in hot water, to be in trouble.
> *faire de l'argent comme de l'eau* – to make a lot of money. *Lit.* to make money like water.
> *faire eau* – to leak (water).

Écartant : *adj.* – disorienting. Typically used to describe an area in which it's easy to become lost.

Écarter : *v.t.* – to lose (something).

> *J'ai écarté ma montre* – I lost my watch.

(s')Écarter : *v.i.* – to lose one's way, to become disoriented.

> *Je m'écarte chaque fois que je marche dans ce coin-là.* – I get lost every time I walk around that area.
> *Elle est pas mal écarté* – She's pretty lost.

Écartillé(e) : *adj.* – with legs spread apart.

> *Je l'ai trouvé tout écartillé dans la neige.* – I found him spread-eagled in the snow.

Échapper : *v.t.* – 1. *Fr.* to escape 2. to drop, to let go.

> *J'ai échappé mon crayon par terre.* – I dropped my pen on the floor.
> *échapper une occasion* – to lose an opportunity.

(s')Échapper : *v.i.* – 1. to be indiscreet. 2. To lose one's cool, to become angry.

Échouer : *v.t.* – to fail (a test, etc.).

Écœurant : *adj.* – 1. amazing, phenomenal, out of this world. 2. Disgusting.

> *C'est un film écœurant !* – It's an amazing film!
> *Je trouvais son attitude écœurante.* – I found his attitude to be disgusting.

Écœurer★ : *v.t.* – to piss off, to bother, to annoy.

> *Il m'a écœuré toute la nuit, ce gars-là.* – That guy annoyed me the whole night.

École : *n.f.* – *Fr.* school.

> ❧ *école de rang* – country(side) school.
> ❧ *foxer l'école* – to play hooky, to cut school.

Écornifler : *v.i.* – to snoop, to peep, to spy on.

Écornifleur(euse) : *n.m. /fem.* – snooper, peeping tom.

Écourtiché : *adj.* – very short (for clothes).

Écouter : *v.t.* – 1. *Fr.* to listen. 2. to watch (a movie, television, etc.). 3. to obey, to pay attention to.

> *On a écouté un très bon film hier.* – We watched a great film yesterday.
> *Il faut que tu m'écoutes !* – You have to listen to me!
> ❧ *écouter la musique à planche* – to listen to very loud music. *Lit.* to listen to music flat-out.
> ❧ *écouter une vue* – to watch a movie.

Écrapouti(e) : *adj.* – crushed, collapsed.

Écrapoutir : *v.t.* – to collapse, to breakdown.

(s')Écraser : – *v.t.* – *to crash out, to relax.*

   On s'est écrasé sur le divan. – *We crashed out on the sofa.*

Efface : *n.f.* – eraser.

Effoirer : *v.t.* – to crush, to flatten.

(s') Effoirer : *v.t.* – to crash (out), to collapse.

   Après la partie, on s'est effoirés chez lui. – After the party, we crashed at his place.

Effrayant : *adj.* – 1. *Fr.* incredible, disturbing, terrible 2. surprising, incredible, extraordinary.

   C'est effrayant comment qu'elle croit tout ce qu'il dit. – It's incredible how she believes everything he says.

Égal : *adv.* – *equally, in equal measure.*

   partager (quelque chose) égal. – *to split (something) equally.*

Égarouillé(e) : *adj.* – wild, crazed.

   Il me regardait avec des yeux égarouillés. – He looked at me with wild eyes.

(s')Éjarrer : *v.i.* – 1. to crash out, to spread out. 2. to attempt to do several things at once (without success).

   En arrivant chez moi, j'ai trouvé mon fils éjarré dans le *fauteuil.* – Upon arriving home, I found my son crashed out on the sofa.

Embarquer : *v.i.* – to get in, get on, join.

Veux-tu embarquer avec moi ? – Do you want to ride with me? (*impl.* in a car).

On va tous embarquer sur le projet ensemble. – We're going to join the project all together.

🌿 *embarquer quelqu'un sur le pouce* – to pick up someone hitchhiking.

Embarré(e) : *adj.* – locked in, closed in.

Je me suis fait embarrer au bureau. – I got myself locked in the office.

(s')Emmieuter : *v.i.* – to become nicer weather, to clear off.

Selon lui il devrait s'emmieuter après midi – According to him, it should clear off after noon.

(s')Empironner : *v.i.* – to become worse weather, to sock in.

(pour) Emporter : *v.t.* – to take out, to go.

Je prendrais deux cafés pour emporter, s'il vous plaît. – I'd like two coffees to go, please.

En autant que... : *Expr.* – Insofar as...

En bas de... : *Expr.* – beneath.

(C'est) En plein ça : *Expr.* – (That's) pretty much it, (That's) completely the case.

En tout temps que... : *Expr.* – Anytime that.

Encan : *n.m.* – auction.

(s')Endormir : *v.t.* – 1. Fr. to go to sleep. 2. to be sleepy, to doze off.

Je m'endormais derrière le volant. – I was asleep at the wheel.

Endurer : *v.t.* − to put up with, to endure.

Je ne peux plus l'endurer. − I can't stand him anymore.

Ènéoué : *expr.* − anyway, anyhow. *Def. Eng.* Anyway.

(s')Énerver : *v.i.* − to get upset.

🌿 *s'ennerver le poil des jambes* − to get upset. *Lit.* "to excite one's leg hair".

Enfarge : *n.f.* − obstacle.

(s')Enfarger : v.i. − 1. to become tangled up in, to get stuck in (something). 2. to trip.

🌿 *s'enfarger dans les fleurs (du tapis)* − to become mired in the details. (*Lit.* to become caught up in the (carpet) flowers).

(se faire) Énfirouaper : *expr.* − to get led along, to get taken.

Enlever : *v.t., v.i.* − *Fr.* to remove, to take off.

🌿 *enlever une pelure* − to remove one's coat *Lit.* to take off a layer.

Engagé(e) : *adj.* − in use, taken.

La ligne est engagée. − The line is busy.

Engraisser : *v.i.* − to gain weight.

Enmieuter : *v.i.* − to get better, to improve.

Ennuyance : *n.f.* − annoyance.

Ennuyant(e) : *adj.* − tiring, boring, annoying.

Ennuyeux (euse) : *adj.* − *Fr.* tiring, boring, annoying.

Enregistreuse : *n.f.* – tape recorder.

Enteka : *expr.* – anyhow, in any case. *Def.* En tout cas.

Entre autres : *expr.* – *Among other things.*

Envoye donc! : *expr.* – C'mon, then!

Enwaille (donc)! : *expr.* – *sl.* C'mon! Move your butt! *Def. Envoye donc!*

Épais(se) : *adj. & N. masc/fem.* – 1. thick-skulled (person). 2. fool, idiot, numskull.

    Ce gars là est un épais. – That guy is a numskull.

Épaisseur : *adj. & n.m.* – *Fr.* thickness.

    (s'habiller en) epaisseurs – (to dress) in layers. *Lit.* "to dress in thicknesses".

Épaté : *adj.* – *impressed.*

Épater : *v.t.* – *to impress.*

    épater la gallerie – *to make a grand entrance.*

Épeurant : *adj.* – fear-causing, scary.

Épeurer : *v.t.* – to scare, frighten.

Épicerie : *n.f.* – shop

    faire l'épicerie – to go (food) shopping.

Épinette : *n.f.* – spruce (gum), as used for its medicinal qualities (i.e. as a sedative, aid for digestion, etc).

    bière d'épinette – root beer.

Épingle : *n.f.* – pin, holder.

    épingle à linge – clothespin.

Épinglette : *n.f.* – brooch, pin.

Épivarder : *v.t.* – to reprimand, to scold.

(s')Épivarder : *v.i.* – 1. *sl.* to take a breather, to get out a bit. 2. to spread oneself too thin.

Épluchette : *n.f.* – corn-husking party, in which guests husk and cook corn as a part of the festivities.

Épouvant(e) : *adj.* – incredible, unbelievable.

    àller à l'épouvant – to go at full speed.

Épouvantable : *adj.* – atrocious.

Épuisé : *adj.* – *Fr.* burned out, extremely tired.

Escalier roulant : *n.m.* – escalator.

Escousse : *n.f.* – a while, a period of time. *Def.* secousse.

Espadrille : *n.f.* – sneakers, sports shoes.

Espérer : *v.i.* – 1. *Fr.* to hope. 2. to wait for.

Espère-moi sur le coin, j'arrive. – Wait for me on the corner, I'll be right there.

Essence : *n.f.* – flavor, taste, smell.

Essuie-vitre : *n.m.* – winshield wiper.

Estimé : *n.m.* – estimate, price quote.

Et : *art. – Fr.* And.

  🌭 *Et un chausson avec ça ? – equiv.* "Would you like fries with that?". *Lit.* "And an (apple) pie with that?"

Étampe : *n.f. –* stamp, symbol.

Étamper : *v.t.–* to stamp.

Étage : *n.m. – Fr.* floor, stage. Note that in Québec the first floor of a building is called « *premier étage* », whereas in France it would be called « *rez-de-chaussée* ».

Été des Indiens : *expr. –* Indian summer.

Être : *v.t., v.i. –* to be.

  🌭 *être assis sur son steak –* to be in a comfortable financial position. *Lit.* seated upon (one's) steak.
  🌭 *être d'avance –* to be positive, to be forward-looking.
  🌭 *être sur le B.S.(Bien-être Social) –* to be on welfare.
  🌭 *être en balloune –* to be pregnant.
  🌭 *Être une bine –* to be nothing, to be small.
  🌭 *être (bien) blond –* to be dumb. *Lit.* to be (very) blond.
  🌭 *être de bonne heure sur le piton –* to be up at the crack of dawn. *Lit.* to be on the button early.
  🌭 *être bossu –* to be skilled in business.
  🌭 *être sur la brosse –* to be smashed, to be drunk. *Lit.* to be on the brush.
  🌭 *être dans le champ –* to be in error, to be mistaken. *Lit.* to be in the field.
  🌭 *être ben chum avec (quelqu'un) –* to be really chummy with (someone)
  🌭 *être à coté de la track –* to be in error, to make a mistake. *Lit.* to be next to the (train) track.

être au coton – 1. to be at the end of one's means or patience. 2. to be exhausted.

être tout croche – to be bad, to be dirty, to be distasteful.

être sur la décrisse★ – to be wrecked, to be in a piteous state.

(ne pas) être la fin du monde – to (not) be the end of the world.

être à main – 1. to be friendly, obliging. 2. to be close, right at hand.

être dans l'eau bouillante (chaud) – to be in hot water, to be in trouble.

être dans le jus – to be swamped, to be busy. *Lit.* to be in the juice.

être dans les patates – to be in error, to be mistaken. *Lit.* to be in the potatos.

être dans la lune – to be spaced out. *Lit.* to be on the moon.

être de la petite bière – to be without importance. *Lit.* to be of small beer.

être en boisson – to be drunk.

être en tabarnac★★ – *sl.* to be pissed off, to be upset.

être capable (de) – to be able (to do something).

être chaud – to be drunk, *sl.* to be lit.

être en crisse★★ – to be pissed off, to be upset.

être en (beau) joualvert – to be furious

être aux femmes – to be homosexual (for a woman).

être game – to be willing, to be game.

être bien gréyé – to be all set, to be ready.

être habillé comme lachienne à Jacques – to be badly dressed. *Lit.* to be dressed like Jacques' dog.

être aux hommes – to be homosexual (for a man).

être ketchup – 1. to be easy 2. to be complete.

être mieux de… – to be better to…

être mort de rire – 1. to be dying (of laughter) 2. to be all set, to be guaranteed success.

être né pour un petit pain – born to be mediocre. *Lit.* to be born for a little bread.

❋ *être parlable* – to be able to be talked with.

❋ *être rond comme une bine* – to be completely sloshed (drunk). *Lit.* "to be as round as a bean".

❋ *être sur le party* – to be in party-mode, to be on a bender.

❋ *être à pic* – to be grumpy, irritable.

❋ *être à pied* – to be in financial difficulty. Opposite sense from English "to be on one's feet" (to be financially independent).

❋ *être pogné sur (quelqu'un)* – to be stuck on (someone)

❋ *être pour (quelque chose)* – to be in favor of (something), to be for (something).

❋ *être dans le rouge* – to be in the red, to be in financial difficulty.

❋ *être dans le rush* – to be in a rush.

❋ *être supposé de…* – to be supposed to…

❋ *être en tabarnac*✶✶ – to be pissed off, to be upset.

❋ *être dans le trou* – to be in trouble. *Lit.* to be in a hole

Étrivant : *adj.* – annoying, teasing.

Étriver : *v.t.* – to tease, to annoy, to perturb.

Eux-Autres : *pron.*– they, them.

(s') Evacher : *v.i.* – to crash out, to relax.

(s') Evader : *v.i.* – to leave, to disappear.

(s') Exciter : *v.i.* – *Fr.* to become excited.

❋ *s'exciter le poil des jambes* – to get upset. *Lit.* "to excite one's leg hair"

Excusez ! : *expr.* – Excuse me!

Extensionner : *v.t.* – to prolong, to extend.

J'ai fait réparer mon moteur, ça va extensionner un peu combien (de temps) ça dure. – I just had my motor fixed, that should make it last a bit longer.

F

Face : *n.f.* − *Fr.* face, front.

❧ *avoir la face à terre* − to be annoyed, to be vexed.
❧ *avoir un face de bœuf* − to be in a bad mood. *Lit.* to have a face of beef.
❧ *(une) face à fesser dédans* − a hateful face.

Fâchant(e) : *adj.* − irritating, annoying, bothersome.

Facture : *n.m.* − bill, tab. *Lit.* invoice.

Fafoin : *adj.* − idiot, fool (for a person)

❧ *faire en fafoin* − to screw up, to do badly.

Faire : *v.i., v.t.* − 1. *Fr.* to do, to make. 2. to seem, to appear.

❧ *Ça fait !* − that'll do!
❧ *Ça va faire* − that will do, that's enough.
❧ *faire l'affaire* − to be sufficient, to do the job.
❧ *faire un air bête* − to look (at someone) with contempt.
❧ *(se) faire aller* − to hurry up.
   Ay, fais-toi aller, la réunion commence dans trois minutes − Hurry it up − the meeting starts in three minutes!
❧ *faire ami(e) (avec quelqu'un)* − to become friends (with someone).
❧ *faire application* − to apply (*Ex.* for a job).
❧ *faire des accroires* − to make (someone) believe something untrue, to decieve someone.
❧ *(se) faire amancher* − to be had, to be taken advantage of.
❧ *faire de l'argent comme de l'eau* − to make a lot of money *Lit.* to make money like water.
❧ *faire attention à (quelqu'un)* − take care of (one's) self.
❧ *se faire avoir* − to be had, to be taken advantage of.

faire du barda – to be noisy.

se faire bumper – to get bumped out, to be pushed aside.

faire la baboune – to pout.

faire le bec fin – to be fussy about what one eats.

faire sa bosse – to make a bundle (of money). *Lit.* to make one's bump.

se faire botter le cul ★ – to get kicked in the ass.

faire le gros bec – to pout. *Lit.* to make a big face.

faire un boute – *sl.* to blow out of somewhere, to leave, to depart.

faire de la broue – to blow hot air, to talk big. *Lit.* to make suds.

faire un canular – to set up a (hidden) candid camera.

faire chier – to suck, to be bad.

faire la commande – to go (food) shopping.

faire coton – to be pathetic.

faire danser les dentiers – to knock someone's lights out. *Lit.* to make someone's teeth dance.

faire du diguidi ha ha – 1. to screw around (joking sense). 2. To screw around (sexual sense)

faire le drôle – to clown around.

faire dur – 1. to be in a bad situation or state, to be rough. 2. To be idiotic, ridiculous, ugly, or crazy. 3. To be badly dressed.

faire eau – to leak (water).

se faire emplir – to be screwed over, to be taken advantage of (by a person or situation)

faire dur – to be in a bad situation or state, to be rough.

(se) faire enfirouaper – to get screwed over, to get taken.

faire l'épicerie – to go (food) shopping.

faire en fafoin – to screw up, to do badly.

faire faire (quelque chose) – to have (something) done.
Je vais le faire faire. – I'm going to have it done.
Je vais t'en faire faire ! – I'm going to do you in!

faire fitter – to adjust.

faire la galette – to make (a lot of) money.

* *(se) faire mettre*** – to get laid, to have sex (with someone).
* *faire à mitaine* – to do by hand. *Lit.* to do by mitten.
* *faire mononcle* – to be old-fashioned, to seem old-fashioned.
* *(se) faire monter les oreilles* – to get a haircut. *Lit.* "to get one's ears lifted".
* *faire le motton* – to make bucks, to make money.
* *faire opérer* – to make (something) work.
* *faire les cent pas* – to pace (back and forth). *Lit.* to do the hundred paces.
* *faire opérer* – to make (something) function, to make (something) work.
* *faire la palette* – to make a lot of money.
* *faire patate* – to fail. *Lit.* to make potatos.
* *faire patienter* – to make (someone) wait.
* *faire le piastre* – to make bucks, to make a lot of money.
* *faire un pli* – to be bothered or upset by something.
* *(se) faire pleumer* – to get taken, to be had. *Lit.* to get plucked.
* *faire du pouce* – to hitchhike.
* *faire (son) rapport à (quelqu'un)* – to (make one's) report to (someone).
* *(se) faire rentrer dedans* – 1. to be hit (by a vehicle or object) 2. to be scolded or otherwise verbally berated
* *faire une saucette* – to go for a dip (in a pool, etc.).
* *faire semblant* – to pretend.
* *faire du (bon) sens* – to make (good) sense.
* *faire son smatte* – to show off.
* *faire du snow* – to snowboard.
* *(se) faire taper les foufounes* – to get a spanking.
* *faire tata* – to wave goodbye.
* *faire un téléphone* – to place a call.
* *faire du temps* – to do time (in prison).
* *Fais-toi-s'en pas.* – Don't worry about it.
* *faire des yeux de porc frais* – to be wide-eyed. *Lit.* "to have eyes like a fresh pig".

(se) Faire à croire : *v.i.* – to make believe, to pretend

Faisable : *adj.* – possible, do-able.

✄ *être faisable* – to be doable.

(Ça) Fait que... : *expr.* – so, that's why.

Il était fatigué, fait qu'on est rentré plus tôt. – He was tired, so we went home early.

Fait(e) : *adj.* – 1. done, complete. 2. done in, in trouble.

✄ *fait à l'os* – completely finished, completely done. *Lit.* done to the bone.

Il est fait, là. – He's really in trouble now.

Faker : *v.t.* – to fake, to pretend.

Falle : *n.f.* – throat, chest.

✄ *avoir la falle basse* – to have a long face, to be down.

Fantasmer : *v.i.* – to dream (of something).

Faque : *expr.* – *contr.* fait que (so, that's why).

Farce : *n.f.* – joke.

C'est pas des farces ! – It's not a joke!

Fardouches : *n.f. pl.* – underbrush, undergrowth.

Fauché : *adj.* – *sl.* broke, out of money.

Fendant(e) : *n.m. /fem. & adj.* – pretentious, arrogant (person).

Fermer : *v.t., v.i.* − *Fr.* to close, to shut.

    ❧ *fermer (un endroit)* − to close (a place, such as a bar).
    Il est déjà 2 h 45, on va fermer la place ! − It's already 2:45am,
    we're going to close the place!
    ❧ *ferme ta soue !* − shut your trap! *Lit.* Shut your sty.

Fesse : *n.f.* − *sl.* butt, rear-end, hind-quarters.

    ❧ *jouer au fesses*★ − to screw, to have sex with (someone).

Fesser : *v.i.* − 1. to strike, to hit head-first. 2. to have a kick, to be
strong. Often used to describe a beverage, etc.

    Lui, il a fessé dans le mur. − He bashed (head-first) into the wall.
    Aye, ça fesse, ta boisson ! − Hey, your drink really has a kick!
    ❧ *(une) face à fesser dédans* − a hateful face.
    ❧ *fesser dans le dash* − to be surprising, to be unexpected.

Fête : *n.f.* − 1. *Fr.* party. 2. birthday.

Fête de la Reine : *n.f.* − (Queen) Victoria day.

Fête du Travail : *n.f* − Labor day.

Fève : *n.f.* − *Fr.* bean.

    ❧ *fèves au lard* − baked beans.

Feu : *n.m.* − *Fr.* fire.

    ❧ *avoir le feu au cul*★ − to be furious. *Lit.* to have fire in the ass.
    ❧ *avoir le feu au passage*★ − to be furious. *Lit.* to have fire in the
    passage.
    ❧ *mouche à feu* − lightning bug, firefly.
    ❧ *vente de feu* − fire-sale

Fier-pet : *adj. & n.m. /fem.* − proud, vain.

Fif, Fifi : *n.m. & adj.* – 1. homosexual (in attitude or action). Only used in the masculine. 2. *sl.* fraidy-cat, chicken.

Filer : *adj.* – to feel (well).

Non, je file pas bien, là. – No, I don't feel very well right now.

Filière : *n.f.* – filing cabinet.

Film de cul : *expr.* – porno film.

Fin(e) : *adj.* – kind, sweet, likeable, gentle, nice, generous.

Il est tellement fin, ce gars-là ! – He's such a great guy!

Fin : *n.f.* – Fr. end.

  fin de semaine – weekend.
  fin de soirée – (rest of) the evening.
  Bonne fin de soirée ! – Have a good evening!

Finissant(e) : *n.m /f.* – graduating student.

  Album des finissants – yearbook.

Fitter : *v.t.* – to fit, to go (together).

Tout ça ne pourrait jamais fitter ensemble. – All that could never go together.
  faire fitter – to adjust.
  Attends, je vais le faire fitter un peu mieux. – Hold on, I'm going to adjust it a bit further.

Flagger : *v.t.* – to hail, to flag (down).

  flagger un taxi – to hail a cab.

Flagosse : *n.f.* – small problem or issue.

Flagosser : *v.i.* – to waste time, to do unimportant things.

Flanc-mou : *adj. & n.m./fem.* – lazy (person).

    grand flanc-mou – good-for-nothing.

Flancher : *v.i.* – *Fr.* to fail, to go out of service.

Flash : *n.m.* – idea, thought.

Je viens d'avoir un flash. – I just had a thought.

Flasher : *v.i.* – to occur to (someone).

Juste après, l'idée m'a flashé. – Just afterwards, the idea occurred to me.

Flot : *n.m./*fem. – child.

Oui, on a des flos à la maison. – Yes, we have kids at home.

Flopper : *v.i.* – to fail, to flop.

Flusher : *v.t.* – 1. to flush (a toilet). 2. To break up with, or drop (a relationship). 3. To fire.

Ils sortent plus ensemble, elle l'a flushé il y a trois jours. – They're not going out any more – she dumped him three days ago.

Flux : *n.m* – diarrhea.

Flyé : *adj.* – extravagant, extreme, *sl.* fly. Generally used to describe a person.

Focusser (sur) : *v.i.* – to focus (on).

Foin : *n.m.* – money.

Foirer : *v.i.* – 1. to party, to have fun. 2. *sl.* to tank, to fail.

Ça va foirer complètement après – That's going to completely tank afterwards.

Folie furieuse : *n.f. /expr.* − mad panic.

C'était la folie furieuse au bureau pour le quart d'heure avant son arrivé − It was a mad panic in the office for the fifteen minutes before he arrived.

Follerie : *n.f.* − silliness, crazy thing.

J'ai fait une follerie − j'ai achété une bouteille de Château d'Yquem pour son anniversaire ! − I did something silly − I bought him a bottle of Château d'Yquem for his birthday.

Forçant(e) : *adj.* − difficult, requiring force.

Formule–1 : *adj. & n.f.* − the best, top-notch. Reference to the annual Formula-1 race held in Montréal.

Fort(e) : *adj.* − *Fr.* strong.

🔹 *boire du fort* − to drink alcohol. *Lit.* to drink some strong (stuff).

Fortiller : *v.i.* − to move non-stop, to twitch.

Fou : *adj.* − *Fr.* crazy, insane.

🔹 *fou bracque* − completely nuts.
🔹 *fou raide* − completely nuts.

Foufounes★ : *n.f.* − *sl.* butt, backside, rear-end.

🔹 *(se) faire taper les foufounes* − to get a spanking.

Fouille : *n.m.* − fall, spill.

🔹 *prendre une fouille* − to take a fall.

Fouler : *v.i.* − to shrink, to pull back.

Fournaise : *n.m.* − furnace, heating system.

Fourneau : *n.m.* − oven.

Fourrant : *adj.* − confusing, annoying, inconvenient, bad.

Fourré : *adj.* − confused, screwed-up.

(se) Fourrer★★★ : *v.t., v.i.* − 1. *sl.* to screw up, to err. 2. *sl.* to screw (sexual sense).

> ❧ *fourrer le chien* − to mess things up. *Lit.* to screw the dog.
> *Je me suis fourré avec cette affaire-là.* − I screwed myself with that deal.

Foxer : *v.t.* − to cheat, to abscond.

> ❧ *foxer l'école* − to play hooky, to cut school.
> ❧ *Foxer un cours* − to skip a class.

(appel à) frais viré : *adj.* − collect call.

Franchement! : *expr.* − really!

Frapper : *v.t., v.i.* − *Fr.* to hit, to strike.

> ❧ *frapper dans le beurre* − to blow it, to miss one's chance.
> ❧ *frapper un nœud* − to hit a wall, to encounter a significant obstacle.

Freaker : *v.i.* − *sl.* to freak (out), to panic.

> *L'affaire m'a fait freaker pendant au moins une semaine.* − The whole deal freaked me out for at least a week.

Frencher : *v.t., v.i.* − to tongue/french kiss.

Frette : *adj.* − cold. (*Def.* froid*).*

   péter au frette − to drop dead. *Lit.* "to stop cold".

(une) Frette : *n.f.* − *sim.* "a cold one" (referring to beer).

On va aller se boire une frette − We're gonna go drink a cold one.

Frigidaire : *n.m.* − refrigerator.

Friler : *v.i.* − to shiver, to tremble (with cold, etc.)

Frileux(-euse) : *adj.* − quick to be cold. Generally said of a person.

Ma blonde est vraiment frileuse − My girlfriend gets cold really quickly.

Fripé : *adj.* − wiped out, *sl.* wasted.

À cause du party, j'étais tout fripé le lendemain − Because of the party, I was pretty wiped out the next morning.

Friper : *v.i.* − to waste.

Friperie : *n.f.* − second-hand (clothing) store.

Froque : *n.f.* − coat.

Frosté : *adj.* − *sl.* wiped out, *sl.* out of it.

Après avoir passé toute la nuit au travail, j'étais pas mal frosté. − After spending all night at work, I was pretty zoned out.

Fru : *adj.* − frustrated. (*Contr.* frustré).

Frustré : *adj.* − *Fr.* upset, frustrated, annoyed.

Frustrer : *v.i.* − *Fr.* to upset, to frustrate, to annoy.

Ça me frustre un peu de ne pas pouvoir y aller. − It frustrates me a bit not to be able to go.

Fuck Friend★ : *n.m.* − lover, casual sex partner.

Fuck off!★★ : *expr.* − "Screw it!", "The hell with it, then!". Not generally a comment directed at a person, but instead the dismissal of a situation or intent.

> *Il y a trop de monde; fuck off, on reviendra demain.* − There're too many people − screw it, let's come back tomorrow.

Fucké★★ : *adj.* − *sl.* screwed up, *sl.* fucked up. A less vulgar and visceral sense than in English.

- *fucké au boutte* − completely screwed up.
- *fucké ben raide★★* − completely screwed up. *Lit.* screwed good and stiff.
- *fucké dans la tête* − screwed up in the head, messed up.
  La situation est fuckée au boutte. − The situation is completely screwed up.

Fucker★★ : *v.t.* − *sl.* to screw up, *sl.* to fuck up.

- *fucker le chien* − 1. to screw around 2. to have difficulty doing something.

Full : *adj., adv.* − completely, very, fully.

> *Moi, j'ai full d'affaires à faire* − I have lots of work to do.
> *Maman, le frigo est full vide !* − Mom, the fridge is completely empty!
- *à full pine* − at full speed.

Fun : *n.m.* – fun, enjoyment.

Hé ! c'est le fun, ça ! – Hey, that's cool!

　avoir du fun – to have fun, to have a good time.
　　On va avoir du fun demain. – We're going to have a good time tomorrow.

　(un) fun noir – a crazy good time.

　pour le fun – for the fun of it, not serious.
　　Je ne voulais pas vraiment leur deranger – c'était juste pour le fun – I didn't really mean to bother them – it was just for the fun of it.

Funerailles : *n.f. pl.* – funeral

G

Galerie : *n.f.* – balcony, terrace.

Galette : *n.f.* – *Fr.* biscuit, shortbread.

   ❧ *faire la galette* – to make (a lot of) money.

Galon : *n.m.* – measuring tape.

Galvaude : *n.f.* – poutine (french fries and lumps of cheese covered in gravy) mixed with chicken and peas.

Galvauder : *v.i.* – 1. to tease, to flirt, to pursue the opposite sex. 2. to botch a job.

Galvaudeux(-euse) : *n.m. /fem.* – one who gallantly pursues opposite sex.

Game : *adj* – willing, prepared

   ❧ *Être game* – to be game, to be willing

Gant : *n.m.* – glove.

   ❧ *laisser tomber les gants* – to "take the gloves off". *Lit.* "forget about the gloves".

   ❧ *mettre des gants blancs* – to handle with kid gloves, to treat gently.

Garde ! : *expr.* – look! (imperative, *Contr.* regarder*)*.

   ❧ *Garde donc !* – Look at that!
     Garde, je n'ai plus le temps pour ça. – Look, I don't have time for this anymore.

Garde-robe : *n.m.* – closet, wardrobe.

   sortir du garde-robe – to come out of the closet, to reveal one's homosexuality.

Gardon : *expr.* – "Look, then". *Def.* regarde, donc.

   Gardon, il faut que je te parles ! – Look, I gotta talk with you.
   Gardon ça ! – Check that out!

Garderie : *n.f.* – *Fr.* daycare center.

Gardien(ne) : *n.masc. /fem.* – *Fr. babysitter.*

Garnotte : *n.f. /n.f. pl.* – 1. pebble. 2. gravel.

Garnotter : *v.t.* – to whip or throw something (at something/ someone).

Garrocher : *v.t.* – 1. to toss, throw, or project something. 2. to work quickly or carelessly.

   Les enfants garrochaient des roches au chien. – The children threw rocks at the dog.

Gars : *n.m.* – *Fr.* guy. Used in the possessive *(mon gars)* to add emphasis when speaking with someone, in somewhat the same sense as *sl.* "dude" or *sl.* "man" in English.

   Là, mon gars, j'étais complètement crevé. – At that point, dude, I was totally exhausted.

Gaspille : *n.m.* – waste.

Gâté : *adj.* – spoiled

Gâter : *v.i.* – to spoil (someone).

Gaz : *n.m.* – *Fr.* gas, fuel.

Gazer : *v.t.* – to fill up (with gas).

Gelé : *adj.* – 1. *Fr.* frozen. 2. *sl.* stoned, *sl.* baked (from drugs).

Geler : *v.i.* – to be freezing, to be cold.

Moi, je gele, là. – Well, I'm freezing.

Gênant(e) : *adj.* – *Fr.* intimidating, blocking, causing hesitation.

Je trouvais son attitude un peu gênante. – I found his attitude somewhat intimidating.

Gêné : *adj.* – shy, hesitant, nervous.

Je suis gêné de parler à mon patron à ce sujet. – I'm hesitant to talk with my boss about that.

Genre : *n.m., expr.* – 1. *Fr.* kind of, type. 2. *sl.* like. The latter usage is almost identical to the slang American use of the word *like* in casual speech.

C'est le genre de gars qui ferait ça. – He's the kind of guy who'd do that.

C'est est un gars cool, genre. – He's, like, a cool guy.

Gérant(e) : *n.m/f.* – manager.

Gicleur : *n.m.* – fire sprinkler.

Gigoter : *v.i.* – to hurry up, to move quickly.

Gilet : *n.m.* – light shirt (especially a sports shirt).

Gîte (touristique) : *n.m.* – Bed & Breakfast (B&B).

Gizmut : *n.m.* – *sl.* gizmo.

Glace : *n.f.* – ice cube.

Glandouneux(euse) : *adj. & n.m./fem.* – lazy oaf, do-nothing, slacker.

Gnochon(ne) : *adj. & n.m./f.* – ignoramus, uneducated (person).

Goaler : *v.i.* – 1. to act as a goalie (soccer). 2. to work very hard.

Goaleur : *n.m.* – goalie.

Gossage : *n.m.* – fooling around, a waste of time.

Gogosse : *n.f.* – small (cheap or unimportant) object.

Gomme : *n.f.* – 1. *Fr.* pencil eraser. 2. chewing gum.

Gosser : *v.i.* – 1. to fiddle with, to fool with (something) 2. to waste time on the details. 3. to bug, to bother.

Gosse de robot : *n.m.* – teaball.

Gosses★ : *n.f.* – 1. *Fr.* children. 2. testicles.

> *avoir des gosses★* – *sl.* to have balls, to be brave.
> *partir sur une gosse★* – to leave (somewhere) quickly. *Lit.* "to leave on a testicle".

Gosseux(euse) : *adj. & n.m./fem.* – 1. Someone who likes to fiddle around with things. 2. a big talker, one who thinks him/herself bigger than their breeches.

Gougounes : *n.f.* – beach sandals.

Goût : *n.m.* – *Fr.* taste.

> *avoir le goût (de faire quelque chose)* – to feel like (doing something).
> *J'ai le goût de faire l'amour.* – I feel like making love.

Grafigne : *n.f.* – scratch.

Grafigner : *v.t.* – 1. to scratch, to graze. 2. to mar, to damage.

Il s'est fait grafigner par son frère. – He was scratched by his brother.
S'il continue de même, ça va grafigner ma réputation. – If he continues this way, it will hurt my reputation.

Grand monde : *expr.* – high society, the upper crust.

Graine★★ : *n.f.* – 1. schlong, penis. 2. Idiot, fool.

Graisser : *v.t.* – to grease (up), to butter. Typically used in cooking.

Graisseuse : *n.f.* – (an) order of french fries. *Lit.* "a greasy"

Grano : *n.m.* – *contr.* Granola

Grano : *adj.* – earthy, homey (usually for a person)

Granola : *n.m.* – health food fanatic.

Gras dur : *expr.* – lucky. *Lit.* hard fat.

Grassette : *adj.* – chubby, overweight (used for a girl or woman)

Son visage est belle, mais est toutefouis un peu grassette – She's visually pretty, but a little chunky even so.

Grassouillette : adj – chubby, overweight (used for a girl or woman)

Gratin : *n.m.* – the who's-who, the upper crust.

Le gratin artistique est venu cette soirée là. – The who's-who of the art world came that evening.

Gratte : *n.f.* – 1. snowplow. 2. hand-held ice scraper.

T'es malchanceux, mon homme, la gratte a déja passé. – You're out of luck, my friend, the snowplow already went by.

Gratte-la-cenne : *n.m.* – miser. *Lit.* cent-scraper.

Gratter : *v.i.* – to be stingey, to be tight-fisted.

Gratteux(-euse) : *n.m./f. & adj.* – (one who is)avaricious; stingy or tight-fisted.

Gratteux : *n.m.* – (scratchable) lottery, ticket.

Gravel : *n.f.* – gravel.

Gréluche : *n.f.* – low-class or unintelligent woman.

Gripette : *adj.* Crabby, Cranky.

   T'es pas mal gripette avant ton café le matin! – You're pretty cranky before your coffee in the morning!

Gruau : *n.m.* – oatmeal, hot cereal.

Gréyé : *adj.* – prepared, equipped, ready.

   être bien gréyé – to be all set, to be ready.

(se) Gréyer : *v.i.* – to prepare, to equip oneself.

Griller : *v.t.* – to tan, to bake in the sun.

Grippe : *n.f.* – *Fr.* the flu.

Grippé : *adj.* – *Fr.* infected with the flu.

Gros(se) : *adj.* – *Fr.* large, big

   gros(se) comme une allumette – as thin as a matchstick.
   gros comme un baril – obese.

Grosse Mol : *expr.* – a large Molson beer.

(se) Grouiller : *v.i.* – to hurry up, to move quickly.

Guedaille : *n.f.* – over-dressed, over-made woman.

Guedille : *n.m.* – hot-dog with sauerkraut.

> ❦ *avoir le guedille au nez* – to have a runny nose.

Guenille : *n.f.* – 1. rag. 2. *n.f.pl* : (cheap) clothes.

> ❦ *À chaque guenille son torchon* – To every girl her guy. *Lit.* to each cloth its rag.

Gueule★ : *n.f.* – *Fr.* maw, mouth (of an animal). Slang reference to one's mouth, or the words which come from it.

> ❦ *avoir la gueule fendue jusqu'aux oreilles.* – to be grinning from ear to ear.

Gugus : *n.m.* – small (cheap or unimportant) object.

Guidoune★★ : *n.f.* – whore, slut.

H

Habit : *n.m.* – suit of clothes.

Je lui ai acheté un bel habit pour Noël. – I bought him a nice suit of clothes for Christmas.

Hab : *n.m.* – *contr.* habitant.

Habiller : *v.t.* – to dress.

 être habillé comme lachienne à Jacques – to be badly dressed. *Lit.* to be dressed like Jacques' dog.

 (s'habiller en) epaisseurs – (to dress) in layers. *Lit.* "to dress in thicknesses".

 (s'habiller en) pelures d'oignons – (to dress) in layers. *Lit.* "to dress in onion skins".

Habitant(e)★ : *adj & n.m. /f.* – redneck, country bumpkin.

Hambourgeois : *n.m.* – hamburger.

Haut : *adj.* – *Fr.* high.

 en haut de – above.

Hein? : *expr.* – What?

Herbe à puce : *n.f.* – poison ivy.

Heure : *n.f.* – *Fr.* hour.

 heures d'affaires – business hours.

Hèvé : *adj.* – difficult, serious. *Eng.* heavy. Note the Québécois usage is generally restricted to description of a weighty or serious situation.

La situation de sa mère est assez hèvé. – Her mother's situation is pretty serious.

Historique : *n.f.* – story, tale.

C'est une historique assez intéressante. – It's a pretty interesting story.

Hiver : *n.m.* – *Fr.* winter.

☙ *Qu'est-ce que ça mange en hiver?* – What is (it) like? *Lit.* What does it eat in wintertime?

Homme : *n. masc* – *Fr.* man. Often used in the possessive (*mon homme*), to add emphasis when speaking with someone, in somewhat the same sense as *sl.* "dude" or *sl.* "man" in English.

Là, mon homme, j'étais complètement crevé. – At that point, dude, I was totally exhausted.

Hostic★ : *expl.* – see *ostic*.

Hostie★★ : *expl.* – see *ostie*.

Horaire : *n.m.* – schedule, timetable.

Veux-tu me vérifier l'horaire? – Would you check the schedule for me?

Hot : *adj.* – high-quality, neat, *sl.* hot.

Il est hot, ton char! – Your car is really hot!

Huard : *n.m.* – dollar.

Huile : *n.f.* – *Fr.* oil.

☙ *baigner dans l'huile* – to go smoothly, to be working okay. *Lit.* "to bathe in oil".
Quant au reste du projet, pour le moment ca baigne dans l'huile – As for the rest of the project, for the moment it's going pretty smoothly.
☙ *huile à bras* – elbow-grease, real effort.

I

Ici : *adv.* – *Fr.* here, in this place.

> ❧ *D'ici…* – Between now and…
> *D'ici un an, il sera fait.* – Within a year, it will be done.

Icitte : *adv.* – here. *Def.* ici.

Idée : *n.f.* – *Fr.* idea.

> ❧ avoir toute son idée – to be clear-minded. Often said of an elderly person who is in full command of their senses.

Il n'y a pas de trouble ! : *expr.* – No worries!

Impassable : *adj.* – unable to be traversed, blocked.

> *Après la tempête de vèrglas, ma rue était impassable pour la moitié d'une semaine* – After the ice storm, my road was blocked off for half a week.

Incontournable : *adj.* – unforseeable, unavoidable.

Inécoutable : *adj.* – unlistenable.

Innocenterie : *n.f.* – silliness, stupidity.

Instantané : *adj.* – dissolvable powder form (such as coffee, soup, etc).

Intéressant(e) : *adj.* – 1. *Fr.* (intellectually) interesting, stimulating. 2. important, a good thing. *N.B.* International French and English only use the former of these two meanings.

> *C'est une histoire intéressante !* – That's an interesting story!
> *Paul ne vient pas, donc ça serait intéressant que tu viennes avec nous.* – Paul isn't coming, so it would be a good thing if you came with us.

Intraduisible : *adj.* – unable to be translated.

Introduire : *v.i.* – *Fr.* to introduce, present. Québécois often use this word (rather than *présenter*) for personal introductions.

Instant (à l') : *n.m.* – right now, at the moment.

Il n'est pas parlable à l'instant. – You can't really talk with him right now.

Il faut que tu le fasses à l'instant où je te le dis. – You need to do it precisely when I tell you.

Itinérant(e) : *n.m. /f.& adj* – homeless (person)

Itou : *conj.* – also.

J

Jack : *n.m.* – Jack.

> *bon Jack* – a good guy.
> *grand Jack* – a big guy.

Jacker : *v.t.* – to jack up, to elevate.

Jamb : *n.f.* – *Fr.* leg

> *s'exciter le poil des jambes* – to get upset. *Lit.* "to excite one's leg hair"

Jambon : *n.m.* – *Fr.* ham, hamhock.

> *(Un) gros jambon* – a self-satisfied individual

Jammé : *adj.* – stuck, jammed.

Jammer : *v.t.* – 1. to jam, to force. 2. *sl.* to jam, to play music improvisationally.

Jaquette : *n.f.* – nightshirt.

Jarnigoine : *n.m/f.* – 1. chatterbox, talkative person. 2. Intelligence, initiative

> *avoir le jarnigoine* – to be intelligent.

Jaser : *v.i.* – to chat with, to speak with (someone).

Ouais, on a jasé hier. – Yeah, we spoke yesterday.

Jasette : *n.f.* – chat, quick conversation.

> *piquer une jasette* – to have a chat.

Jaspiner : *v.i.* – to complain constantly, to lament.

Jaspineux(euse) : *adj & n.m. /fem.* – one who complains constantly.

Jériboire!★ : *expr.* – Heck!, Darn it!

Jésus-Christ!★ : *expl.* – Jesus Christ!

Job : *n.f.* – job, work.
- *ajouter de la job* – to add work (to something)
- *job de bras* – *sl.* gruntwork, labor. *Lit.* arm-work.

Jos★★ : *masc. pl.* – breasts.

Joual : *n.m.* – popular language, slang.

Joualvert★ : *expr.* – Hell!
- *être en (beau) joualvert*★ – to be furious.

Jouer : *v.t., v.i.* – *Fr.* to play.
- *jouer au fesses*★ – to screw, to have sex with (someone).
- *jouer aux quilles* – to bowl, to go bowling.

Joues : *n.m. pl.* – affectionate term for a woman's behind. *Lit.* cheeks.

Journée : *n.f.* – *Fr.* day.
- *avoir sa journée dans le corps* – to have had a rough day. *Lit.* 'to have (his) day in (his) body.'
- *journée off* – vacation day.

Jus : *n.m.* – 1. *Fr.* juice. 2. *Fr.* sauce, stew. 3. electricity, current.
- *être dans le jus* – *sl.* to be swamped, to be busy. *Lit.* to be in the sauce.

Juste : *adj.* – 1. *Fr.* just, right (ethical sense). 2. close to, on the verge
of something.

> *C'est juste un peu trop petit.* – It's just a little too small.
> *C'était juste!* – He just made it!
> ❧ *au juste* – actually.

K

Kaline : *expl.* – *sim.* Dammit! (gentler form of câlisse).

Kessé ça? : *expr.* – What is that? (*Contr. Qu'est-ce que c'est, ça*)

Kétaine : *adj.* – taseless, bad.

> ❧ *Kétaine au boutte.* – completely tasteless.
> *Ses vêtements sont kétaines au boutte.* – His clothes are completely tasteless

Ketchup : *adj., n.m.* – ketchup.

> ❧ *être ketchup* – 1. to be easy 2. to be complete.

Kick : *n.m.* – kick, blow.

> ❧ *avoir un kick sur (quelqu'un)* – to have a crush on (someone).

Kicker : *v.t.* – 1. to kick, propel forward. 2. to complain.

Kif-kif : *adj.* – an equal split, half-and-half

Kioute : *adj.* – cute.

Kodak : *n.m.* – camera.

Kossé? : *expr.* – What is it? *Def.* Qu'est-ce que c'est?

L

Là : *expr.* – 1. *Fr.* there, in that place. 2. now.

 ❧ *Là, là…* – Now about that…

Là-dessus : *conj.* – about it, about that.

Je voudrais bien te parler là-dessus. – I'd like to talk with you about that.
Je vais mettre un homme là-dessus. – I'll put a man on it.

Lâche : *adj* – *Fr.* lazy, laxidasical.

 ❧ *lâche comme un âne.* – lazy as an ass (donkey).

Lâcher : *v.t., v.i.* – 1. to quit, to give up, to let go. 2. to lick. 3. to fail, to give out.

Mon cellulaire va lacher bientôt – My cellphone is going to give out pretty soon.
 ❧ *lâcher un coup de fil* – to give someone a phone call.
 ❧ *lâcher une fiouse* – to fart, to pass wind. *Lit.* To pop a fuse.
 ❧ *lâcher son fou* – to let one's hair down, to let loose.
 ❧ *(se) lâcher lousse* – to let one's self loose (to have fun, etc)
 ❧ *Lâche pas la patate !* – Don't give up ! *Lit.* Don't let go of the potato.
 ❧ *lâcher un pet* – to fart, to pass wind.
 ❧ *lâcher un wack* – to let out a yell.

Laisser Tomber : *v.t., v.i.* – *Fr.* to drop something, to forget about something, to let (something) fall.

 ❧ *laisser tomber les gants* – to "take the gloves off". *Lit.* "to forget about the gloves".

Lambineux (-euse) : *n.m./fem. & adj.* – one who is indecisive or hesitant.

Lancer : *v.t.* – *Fr.* to throw, to launch (something).

    lancer un ballon – to start a rumor, particularly a political one.

Langue : *n.f.* – 1. *Fr.* tongue. 2. *Fr.* language, spoken tongue.

    avoir la langue à terre – 1. to be exhausted. 2. to be very hungry. *Lit.* to have (one's) tongue on the ground.

    avoir la langue sale – to have a dirty mouth. *Lit.* to have a dirty tongue.

    sur le bout de la langue – on the tip of (one's) tongue.

Lavage : *n.m.* – laundry.

J'ai tellement de lavage à faire ! – I have so much laundry to do!

Lave-auto : *n.m.* – carwash.

Laveuse : *n.f.* – washing machine.

Légume : *n.m.* – *Fr.* vegetable.

    la grosse légume – the big cheese (the important person). *Lit.* big vegetable.

Lendemain de veille : *n.m. expr.* – the "morning after" (a party, etc).

Levée de fonds : *n.m./expr.* – fundraising.

Lever : *v.i/v.t* – 1. *Fr.* to lift, to raise. 2. to get out of bed.

    se lever le coude – to have several beers. *Lit.* to lift one's elbow.

    se lever le gros orteil au nord – to get up on the wrong side of the bed, to be cranky. *Lit.* to get up with one's big toe pointed north

    se lever du pied gauche – to get up on the wrong side of the bed, to be cranky. *Lit.* to get up on the left foot.

Lettres carrées : *n.m pl.* – capital letters. *Lit.* square letters.

Lettres moulées : *n.m pl.* – capital (block) letters.

Libre-service : *n.m.* – self-service.

Licencié : *adj.* – license-holder, generally of a liquor license. Restaurants in Québec often display the sign "*Licence complete*" to indicate they sell alcohol.

Lichette : *n.f.* – hickey, red mark left on the skin from a kiss.

Licheux (-euse) : *adj & n.m/f.* – ass-kisser, brown-noser.

Lift : *n.m.* – ride, lift (in a vehicle).

   ❧ *donner un lift* – to give (someone) a lift.
   ❧ *quêteux de lift* – one who incessently seeks out free rides.

Ligne : *n.f.* – 1. *Fr.* waiting line. 2. phone line.

   ❧ *en bout de ligne* – ultimately, finally *(Lit.* at the end of the line).

Limonade : *n.f.* – Lemonade.

Linge : *n.m.* – clothes, or most anything made from material (underwear, sheets, napkins, etc).

   Elle a mis tout son linge dans un sac vert. – She put all his clothes in a garbage bag.

Liqueur : *n.f.* – *Fr.* after-dinner drink.

   ❧ *liqueur douce* – soda, carbonated non-alcoholic drink.

Liseux(euse) : *n.m./fem. & adj.* – bookworm, one who reads constantly.

Lit : *n.m. – Fr.* bed.

- *lit double* – double bed
- *grand lit double* – queen bed.
- *Lit simple* – single bed.
- *très grand lit double* – king bed.

Loadé(e) : *adj.* – 1. loaded (filled). 2. loaded (with money).

Le gars à qui appartient ce char-là, il est pas mal loadé. – The guy who owns that car is pretty loaded.

Loader : *v.t.* – to load, to fill up.

Logis : *n.m.* – *Fr.* apartment, house, place of residence.

Lotion après-rasage : *n.m.* – after-shave lotion.

Loup-marin : *n.m.* – seal. *Lit.* "sea wolf".

Lousse : *adj.& n.m.* – 1. loose, slack, play. 2. generous (in a monetary sense).

Lui, il a toujours été un peu lousse avec son argent. – He's always been pretty generous with his money.

- (se) lâcher lousse – to let one's self loose (to have fun, etc).

Lumière : *n.f.* – 1. *Fr.* light. 2. cars' headlights. 3. traffic light.

Mets tes lumières ! – Put your lights on!
Attention, la lumière va changer ! – Watch it, the light's going to change!

Lunch : *n.m.* – *Eng.* Lunch

- *boîte à lunch* – lunchbox.

Luncher : *v.i.* – to have lunch.

Lyrer : *v.i.* – to whimper.

M

Ma : *Expr.* − I'm going (to…) *Def.* je vais.

Mâchable : *adj.* − chewable.

(se) Maigner (de cul★★) : to hurry up, to move one's ass.

Mal pris : *expr.* − in trouble, in bad shape.

Magané : *adj.* − 1. ruined, battered, wrecked. 2. exhausted.

Je pense que le fauteuil est un peu trop magané pour garder. − I think the couch is a bit too far gone to keep.
J'ai travaillé jusqu'à trois heures du matin, alors là je suis complètement magané. − I was at work 'til three in the morning, so now I'm completely wrecked.

Maganer : *v.t.* − 1. to damage, to cause harm to. 2. to treat something/someone badly.

Je ne veux pas maganer mon veston. − I don't want to damage my suit jacket.

Magasinage : *n.m.* − shopping.

Magasiner : *v.i.* − to go shopping.

Main : *n.f.* − *Fr.* hand.

    avoir les mains pleines de pouces − to be all thumbs.

Maïs soufflé : *n.m.* − popcorn.

(la) Main : *n.f.* − *sl.* main drag, main road in a town.

On s'est promenés sur la main pendant trois heures. − We walked along the main drag for three hours.

Mais que : *Expr.* − As soon as.

Malin(e) : *adj.* − 1. angry 2. nasty, aggressive.

Malle : *n.f.* − mail. *Def. Engl.* mail.

   ❧ *aller à malle* − to go get the mail.

Maller : *v.t.*- to mail, to send.

Manche : *n.f.* − handle.

   ❧ *branler dans le manche* − to hesitate when making a decision.
   Lit. to hesitate in the handle.

Manquer : *v.t., v.i.* − 1. *Fr.* to miss, 2. to barely miss.

   ❧ *J'ai manqué de frapper son char par deux pousses !* − I missed
   hitting his car by two inches!
   ❧ *manquer le bateau* − to miss the boat (figuratively or literally).

Manger : *v.t.* − to eat.

   ❧ *se faire manger* − *sl.* to get chewed out.
   ❧ *en manger une* − *sl.* to 'get it', to get in trouble, to be
   reprimanded. *Lit.* to eat one.
   ❧ *manger (ses) bâs* − 1. to be uncomfortable with one's speech or
   action, *sim.* "open mouth, extract foot". 2. to worry or panic.
   Lit. to eat one's socks.
   ❧ *se laisser manger la laine sur le dos* − to lose one's shirt, to be
   exploited. *Lit.* to let the wool be eaten from your back.
   ❧ *mange de la marde**!* − eat shit!
   ❧ *mange de la schnoute** − eat shit!
   ❧ *Qu'est-ce que ça mange en hiver ?* − What is (it) like? *Lit.* "What
   does it eat in wintertime?".

Marche : *n.f.* − *Fr.* a stroll, a walk.

  ❅ *prendre une marche* − to take a walk.
     On va aller prendre une marche jusqu'à midi. − We're going to go
     for a walk until noon.

Marcher : v.i. − 1. *Fr.* to work, to function properly. 2. *Fr.* to walk.

  ❅ *marcher à mort* − to work beautifully. *Lit.* to work to death.
  ❅ *marcher à planche* − to work perfectly. *Lit.* to work flat-out.

Marde★★ : *n.f., expr.* − shit. (*Def. merde*).

  ❅ *plein de marde★★* − full of shit.
  ❅ *mouche à marde★* − clinger, annoying individual whose
     presence can't be escaped. *Lit.* shit-fly.
  ❅ *tache à marde★* − clinger, annoying individual whose presence
     can't be escaped. *Lit.* shit-stain.

Mardeux : *adj. & n.m./f.* − lucky, fortunate (person).

(se) Marier : *v.t.* − to marry.

Maringouin : *n.m.* mosquito.

Marmaille : *n.f.* − children, kids.

(en) Masse : *n.f.* − 1. a lot of, much of. 2. enough, plenty.

  Ça glisse en masse ! − It's really slippery
  On en a en masse, merci. − We have plenty, thanks.

Matcher : *v.t.* − 1. to put together, to match. 2. To be a match, to fit
together.

  Je n'aurais du jamais le croire, mais le tapis et les draps matchent
  vrainment bien ensemble − I never would have believed it, but the
  rug and drapes really do go well together.

Matrone : *n.f.* – 1. mother-in-law. 2. matron, head of a household.

Mauditement bon : *expr.* – Wickedly good.

Mauditement bon : *expr.* – Wickedly good.

Maususse★ : *expl.* – Moses.

Mautadit : *expl.* – Damn! Softer form of *maudit* (*Fr.* cursed, damned).

Méchant : *adj. & adv.* – 1. *Fr.* wicked, mean, nasty. 2. very, really.

Lui, c'est un gars assez méchant. – He's a pretty mean guy.
Ça va être méchant dur. – That's going to be really hard.

Mèche : *n.f.* – 1. *Fr.* fuse, wick. 2. hair highlights, colored strands.

avoir la mèche courte – to have a short fuse, to be quick-tempered.
Je vais ajouter des mèches bleues demain. – I'm going to add some blue highlights to my hair tomorrow.

Médaille : *n.f.* – coin.

deux côtés de la médaille – *Lit.* both sides of the coin.

(la) Meilleur des mondes : *expr.* – an ideal world.

Mêlant : *adj.* – *Fr.* confusing, disorienting.

C'était mêlant un peu de voir les deux ensemble. – It was a bit confusing to see the two of them together.

Mêlé : *adj.* – *Fr.* confused, mixed up.

(de) Même : *adv.* – like this/that.

Je n'aime pas les gars de même. – I don't like guys like that.

Même à ça : *expr.* – even so.

Mémérage : *n.f.* – gossip, chit-chat.

Mémère : *n.m./fem. & adj.* – talkative, loquacious (person).

Mémérer : *v.i.* – to gossip, to chatter.

Ménage : *n.m.* – *Fr.* housework.

   chicane de ménage – household argument.

Méné : *n.m.* – 1. minnow. 2. person with little weight or influence in a given situation.

   Même s'il est là depuis cinq ans, il est toujours un méné au bureau. – Although he's been there for five years, he still has no influence the office.

Mener : *v.t.* – *Fr.* to lead, to conduct.

   mener le diable – to make a racket, cause a disturbance. *Lit.* to lead the devil.

Menterie : *n.f.* – lie, untruth.

Mer : *n.f.* – *Fr.* sea.

   C'est pas la mer à boire – It's easy. *Lit.* "it's not the (whole) sea to drink".

Messe : *n.f.* – *Fr.* Roman Catholic Mass.

   avoir du monde à la messe – to be crowded. *Lit.* "to have people at the Mass".

Mettre : *v.t.* – 1. *Fr.* to put/place. 2. (se faire) mettre★★★ to get laid, to have sex with someone.

   Mets ça dans ta pipe puis fume ! – Put that in your pipe and smoke it! *Il sortait ce soir juste pour essayer de se mettre*★★★. – He went out tonight just to try and get laid.

❧ *mettre les bars sur les T* – to cross your T's and dot your I's.
❧ *(se) mettre en crisse*★★ – to get pissed-off, to become angry.
❧ *mettre des gants blancs* – to handle with kid gloves, to treat gently.
❧ *mettre la musique dans le tapis* – to play music at high volume. *Lit.* "to put music in the carpet".

Mets-en! : *expr.* – "That's for sure!" *sl.* "Totally"! *Lit.* Add some more.

Miel : *n.m.* – *Fr.* honey.

❧ *mouche à miel* – honeybee.

Mieux : *adj.* – *Fr.* better.

❧ *être mieux de…* – to be better to…
T'es mieux d'aller plus tot – It'd be better for you to go earlier.

Minou : *n.f.* – 1. *Fr.* cat. 2. Darling (term of endearment)

Minoucher : *v.i.* – to caress, to kiss, to cuddle with (someone).

Minoucher : *v.t.* – to flatter (someone), to butter (someone) up.

Minoune : *n.f.* – 1. old car. 2. cat, kitten. Also used as an affectionate word for a young girl.

Oui, ma minoune? – Yes, my darling?

Misère : *n.f.* – difficulty.

❧ *avoir de la misère* – to have difficulty.

Mitaine : *n.f.* – glove, mitten.

❧ *à mitaine* – by hand.
❧ *faire à mitaine* – to do by hand. *Lit.* to do by mitten.

Moffer : *v.i.* − to mess up, to botch, to miss (something).

J'ai essayé lui faire du sushi, mais je l'ai completemment moffé. − I tried to make him sushi, but I completely botched it.

Moine★★ : *n.m.* − 1. *Fr.* monk. 2. *sl.* dick, penis.

Molle : *n.f* − soft ice cream.

Mollo : *adj.* − chilled-out, relaxed.

Monde : *n.m.* − 1. *Fr.* world. 2. *Fr.* people in the world.

    (du) ben bon monde − friendly folk, good people.
    comme du monde − as everyone else (is). *Lit.* "as other folks".

Mononcle : *adj.* − old-style, old-fashioned.

    faire mononcle − to be old-fashioned, to seem old-fashioned.
      Je ne veux pas amener le tapis avec moi, ça fait trop mononcle. − I don't want to bring the carpet, it's too old-fashioned.
      Ouais, ça fait un peu mononcle, mais ce n'est pas grave. − Yeah, it's a bit old-style, but that's not a problem.

Monter : *v.i., v.t.* − *Fr.* to go up, to rise.

    monter d'une coche − to go up a notch, to improve.

Montée : *n.f.* − driveway.

Mordée : *n.f.* − bite.

C'est sûr qu'il a pris une mordée dans ton profit. − It's certain that he took a bite out of your profit.

Mort : *n.f.* − *Fr.* death.

    à mort − a lot, completely.
    Son chien est mort − (*expr*) to be done-in, to be finished. *Lit.* His dog is dead.

Moto hors route : *n.m.* – motocross.

Motoneige : *n.f.* – *Fr.* snowmobile.

Moton : *n.m.* – *Fr.* bump, knot, lump.

🦋 *avoir le moton (dans le gorge)* – 1. to be choked up, to have a lump in one's throat. 2. to be wealthy.
Quand elle lui a dit qu'elle l'aimait, ça se voyait qu'il avait le moton. – When she told him she loved him, you could see how choked up he was.

Motte (de neige) : *n.f.* – snowball.

Mouche : *n.f.* – *Fr.* fly.

🦋 *mouche à cheval* – horsefly.
🦋 *mouche à chevreuil*- deerfly.
🦋 *mouche à feu* – lightning bug, firefly.
🦋 *mouche à marde** – clinger, annoying individual whose presence can't be escaped. *Lit.* shit-fly.
🦋 *mouche à miel* – honeybee.
🦋 *mouche à orignal* – horsefly. *Lit.* "moosefly".

Moufette : *n.m.* – skunk.

Mouillasser : *v.i.* – to drizzle, to sprinkle (light rain).

Mouillassseux : *adj.* – rainy, drizzly.

Mouiller : *v.i.* – 1. *Fr.* to wet. 2. to be rainy, to be wet.

🦋 *mouillir à boire debout* – to be pouring rain. *Lit.* "to rain so you can drink standing up".
Il va mouiller toute la fin de semaine. – It's going to rain the whole weekend.

Moumoune : *adj. & n.m./fem.* – 1. wimp, wuss, fraidy-cat. 2. homosexual.

Moumoute : *n.f.* – hairpiece.

Mourant(e) : *adj.* – hysterical, hilarious.

J'ai vu ce film-là, c'était mourant ! – I saw that film, it was a riot!

Mouton : *n.m.* – *Fr.* sheep.

❧ *revenir à (ses) moutons* – to come back to the subject at hand. *Lit.* to get back to (one's) sheep.

Mouve : *n.m.* – move (allegorical or literal).

C'est un mouve que je ne peux vraiment pas expliquer. – That's a move I really can't explain.

Mouver : *v.i.* – to move (change residences).

Moyens : *n.m. pl.* – *Fr.* the means, the methods, the techniques.

Avez-vous un moyen de le faire livrer chez moi ? – Do you have a way to get it delivered to my place?
Il n'a pas les moyens financiers pour déménager à Westmount. – He doesn't have the financial means to move to Westmount.

MTS : *n.f. pl.* – STD (Sexually-Transmitted Disease). *Abbr.* "*M*aladie *T*ransmise *S*exuellement".

Musique à bouche : *n.f.* – harmonica.

N

Nanane : *n.m.* − 1. candy. 2. treat, goodie.

Elle pleure parce qu'elle n'a pas eu son nanane − She's crying because she didn't get her goodie.

Narc : *n.m.* − drug squad, narcotics law enforcement.

Ne pas valoir de la colle : *expr.* − to be worthless, to be of bad quality. *Lit.* "to not be worth glue".

Necker : *v.i.* − *sl.* to make out, *sl.* to neck, to kiss.

Neige : *n.f.* − *Fr.* snow.

 la neige folle − super-fluffy snow, powder snow.
 motte de neige − snowball.

Neiger : *v.i.* − *Fr.* to snow.

 avoir vu neiger − to have experience. *Lit.* to have seen it snow before.

Neo-Québécois : *n.m/f. & adj* − person recently immigrated to Québec. Effectively the opposite of a Québécois pur-laine.

Nerf : *n.m.* − *Fr.* nerve.

 tomber sur les nerfs − to annoy, to exasperate. *Lit.* to fall upon one's nerves.
 Les nerfs ! − Chill out! Calm down!

Net-fret-sec ! : *expr.* − cut and dry. *Lit.* clean-cold-dry.

Nettoyeur : *n.m.* − dry-cleaner.

(au) Neutre : *adj.* – (in) neutral gear (in a car).

Nez : *n.m.* – *Fr.* nose.

  ❧ *avoir le nez brun* – to be a brown-noser.
  ❧ *respirer par le nez* – to calm down. *Lit.* "to breathe through the nose".

Niaisage : *n.m.* – fooling around, silliness, stupidity.

Niaiseux (-euse) : *n.m./fem., adj.* – idiot(ic), fool(ish).

  T'es ben niaiseux ! – You're a real pain!

Niaiser : *v.i.* – 1. to tease, to annoy. 2. to string someone along, to waste someone's time.

  ❧ *niaiser avec la puck* – to waste time. *Lit.* stop fooling around with the puck.

NIP : *n.m.* – PIN code, password (for a bank machine).

Nœud : *n.m.* – *Fr.* knot.

  ❧ *frapper un nœud* – to hit a wall, to encounter a significant obstacle.

Noirceur : *n.f.* – blackness, darkness.

Nombril du monde : *expr.* – egocentric person. *Lit.* bellybutton of the earth

  ❧ *(se) prendre pour le nombril du monde*- to believe one's self to be the most important thing. *Lit.* to take one's self as the bellybutton of the earth.

Nono : *adj. & n.m./fem.* – idiot, *sl.* bozo.

Noune *** : *n.f.* – reference to female genitalia.

Nounoune : *n. masc. /fem. & adj.* – idiot, imbecile.

Sois pas nounoune, toi ! – Don't be an idiot!

Nounours : *n.m.* – Teddy bear.

Nous–autres : *pron.* – we all, we.

Nouveau(x) : *adj. masc.* – *Fr.* new.

⚜ *attendre du nouveau* – to be expecting a child; to be pregnant. *Lit.* to wait for a new (one).

Nu–bas : *expr.* – in socks. *Lit.* "nude socks".

Objecter : *v.i.* – to object, to oppose.

Occasions : *n.f. pl.* – bargains.

Œuf : *n.m* – *Fr.* egg.

    œufs (au) miroir – eggs "over"
    œufs brouillés – scrambled eggs

Oignon : *n.f.* – *Fr.* Onion.

    (s'habiller en) pelures d'oignons – (to dress) in layers. *Lit.* "to dress in onion skins".

Onguent : *n.m.* – medicinal cream.

    (ne pas être) de l'onguent – to not be expensive. *Lit.* to (not be) medicinal cream.
      Mets-en, c'est pas de l'onguent. – Go ahead (*impl.* add more), it's not that expensive.

O.P.C. : *expr.* – as quickly as possible. *Contr.* au plus crissant.

Opérer : *v.t.* – to make (something) function.

    faire opérer – to make (something) work.

Ordi(n) : *n.m.* – computer *(abbr. ordinateur)*.

Ordinaire : *adj.* – mediocre, of moderate quality.

Orielle : *n.f.* – *Fr.* ear.

    (se) faire monter les oreilles – to get a haircut. *Lit.* "to get one's ears lifted".

Oreilles de Christ : *n.f. pl.* – fried pig ears.

Orignal : *n.m.* – moose.

   ❧ *câler l'orignal* – to throw up, to puke. *Lit.* to call the moose.

Oreille : *n.f.* – *Fr.* ear.

   ❧ *oreilles de crisse* – fried salted pig fat. Traditional Québec dish served in a *cabane à sucre*.
   ❧ *avoir les oreilles dans le crin* – 1. to be careful, fearing something or someone. 2. to be in a bad mood. *Lit.* to have one's ears in horse-hair.

Orteil : *n.m.* – *Fr.* toe.

   ❧ *se lever le gros orteil au nord* – to get up on the wrong side of the bed, to be cranky. *Lit.* to get up with one's big toe pointed north

Ostic★ : *expl.* – softer form of *ostie*.

Ostie★★ : *expl.* – *equiv.* goddam! Derives from the French word for "Host", from the Catholic liturgy.

Ostinage : *n.m.* – argument, disagreement

Ostination : *n.f.* – arguement, disagreement.

(s')Ostiner : *v* – to argue, to disagree.

   C'est sûr qu'il va m'ostiner là-dessus. – It's certain that he'll argue with me about it.

Ostineux(-euse) : *n.m/f & adj.*– argumentative person.

Ou : *prep.* – *Fr.* or, else.

   ❧ *oubedon* – or else (*contr.* ou bien donc).

Ouache! : *excl.* – yuck!

Ouair : *v.t.* – to see (*Def.* voir).

On va ouair un bon show ce soir. – We'll see a good show tonight.

Ouaouaron : *n.m.* – large frog.

Oubedon : *expr.* – otherwise, or else. *Def.* Ou bien donc.

Oublie ça : *expr.* – Forget it.

Ousque : *expr.* – *ou est-ce que* (*Contr. Ou est-ce que*)

Ousquilé? – Where is he?

Oui allô? : *expr. idiom.* – Hello? Used when responding to the telephone.

Ouin : *art.* – yeah.

 ouin pis? – Yeah, and so…?

Oupéllaie! : *expr.* – 1. "Whoa!" 2. "Oups!", "Whoops!"

Ours : *n.m.* – *Fr.* bear

 (un) ours mal-lêché – a scruffy person. *Lit.* a badly-licked bear.

Ouvrage : *n.m.* – work.

P

Pain : *n.m.* – *Fr.* bread.

   être né pour un petit pain – born to be mediocre. *Lit.* to be born for little bread.

Pagette : *n.f.* – pager, beeper.

Pagosse : *n.f.* – thing, object.

Palettes : *n.f. pl.* – front teeth.

Palmarès : *n.m.* – hit list, Top 40.

Pancarte : *n.f.* – sign.

Panneau : *n.m.* – sign.

Pantalon Court : *n.f.* – shorts.

Pantoute : *expr.* – not at all, not entirely (*Def.* pas en toute*)*.

   Pas pire, pantoute ! – Not bad, not bad at all!

Papier sablé : *n.f.* – sandpaper.

Paquet : *n.m.* – a bunch of, a lot of.

   paquet d'affaires – a bunch of things.

Paqueté(e) : *adj.* – 1. loaded, drunk. 2. completely filled, packed. *Lit.* stuffed.

   (se) paqueter la gueule – to get drunk
   (se) paqueter la fraise – to get drunk.

Paquéter : *v.t.* – to pack (bags, etc).

　❄ *paquéter ses petits* – to get ready to leave. *Lit.* "to pack one's little (things)".

(se) Paqueter : *v.i.* – to get loaded, to get drunk.

Par exemple : *expr., prep.* – 1. actually. 2. *Fr.* for example. 3. however, though. The first definition is more common usage:

Je n'y suis pas allé, par exemple. – I didn't go, actually.
Moi, par exemple, je ne suis pas encore convaincu. – I, however, am not yet convinced.

Paraître (bien, mal) : *v.i.* – to appear (well, badly off).

Pardessus : *n.m.* – 1. overcoat. 2. rubbers, boots.

Parcomètre : *n.m.* – parking meter.

Pardessus : *n.m.* – 1. overcoat. 2. rubbers, boots.

Pareil(eille) : *adj.* – 1. *Fr.* same. 2. even so.

　❄ *pareil comme…* – the same as…
Sa mere lui avait dit non, mais elle a fait ça pareil. – Her Mom told her know, but she did it anyway.

(la) Parenté : *n.f.* – extended family (aunts, uncles, cousins, etc).

(pas) Parlable : *adj.* – incommunicative, unable to be spoken with/to.

Il est fâché en ce moment, et donc pas très parlable. – He's mad right now, and so not very communicative.

Parler : *v.i.* – *Fr.* to talk, to speak.

　❄ *parler à travers son chapeau* – to blow hot air, to speak without actual knowledge. *Lit.* "to speak across one's hat".

❧ *parler dans le dos* – to talk behind someone's back.
❧ *parler les baguettes en l'air* – to gesticulate while talking

Parlure : *n.f.* – slang.

Partie des sucres : *n.f.* – party or meal traditionally held at a sugar shack (cabane à sucre) in the springtime.

Partir : *v.i.* – 1. *Fr.* to leave. 2. to start.

On va bientôt partir. – We're going to leave soon.
Veux-tu partir le micro-ondes, s'il te plaît? – Would you start the microwave, please?
❧ *partir en affaires* – to start a business.
❧ *partir pour la gloire* – 1. to head off on a mission. 2. to be pregnant. *Lit.* to head off to glory.
❧ *partir sur une gosse*★ – to leave (somewhere) quickly.
❧ *partir sur une "go"* – to go on a bender, to go all out.

Pas d'affaire! : *expr.* – There's no question!

Pas d'allure : *n.m. /f.* – gauche or maladroit person.

Passage : *n.m.* – corridor, hall.

Passe-Passe : *n.m.* – workaround, alternative method.

(se) Passer : *v.i.* – 1. *Fr.* to pass, pass off. 2. to give, to loan.

As-tu trois dollars à me passer? – Could you loan me three bucks?
❧ *passer sur l'autre bord* – to die.
❧ *passer sur l'autre coté* – to die.
❧ *(se faire) passer (quelque chose) en dessous du nez* – miss a good occasion. *Lit.* to have (something) go right under your nose.
❧ *(se faire) passer un sapin* – to be had, to get a bad deal. *Lit.* to be handed a fir tree.

- *passer au cash* – to get what one deserves.
- *passer au dép(anneur)* – to swing by the convenience store.
- *passer tout droit* – to oversleep. *Lit.* to go right through.
- *passer au feu* – to burn down.
- *passer la nuit ur la corde à linge* – to sleep badly. *Lit.* to sleep on the clothesline.
- *passer proche de (faire quelque chose)…* – to come close to (doing something).
- *se faire passer un citron* – *sl.* to be handed a lemon, to be handed a dud.

Pas-vite : *adj. & n.m. /fem.* – *sl.* slo-mo, slow (person).

Patate : *n.m.* – potato.

- *bebitte à patates* – cockroach.
- *être dans les patates* – to be in error, to be mistaken. *Lit.* to be in the potato (field).
- *patates frites* – french fries.
- *patates pillées* – mashed potatoes.
- *patates de sofa* – couch potato.
- *patates sucrées* – sweet potatoes.
- *Lâche pas la patate !* – Don't give up! *Lit.* Don't let go of the potato.
- *faire patate* – to fail.

Patchée★★ : *adj.* – on the rag, having one's (female monthly) period.

Patcher : *v.t.* – to patch (up), to fix

- *patcher un pneu* – to patch a tire.

Pâte à dents : *n.f.* – toothpaste.

Pâté chinois : *n.m.* – shepherd's pie – an oven-baked pie containing ground beef, corn, and mashed potatoes.

Patente : *n.f.* – thing, object.

- *patente à gosse* – gadget, small object.
- *toute la patente* – the whole bit.

Patenter : *v.t., v.i.* – to patch together, to whip up, to invent.

Patienter : *v.i.* – *Fr.* to wait, to hold on.

On s'excuse de vous avoir fait patienter. – We apologize for the wait.

Patiner : *v.i.* – *Fr.* to skate. Often used to mean "to move" in an allegorical sense.

- *patiner vite* – to skate quickly (literal and figurative senses). *Il faut qu'il patine vite s'il veut réussir.* – He'd better get a move on if he wants to succeed.
- *accrocher ses patins* – to end one's career, give up. *Lit.* to hang up one's skates.

Patof : *n.m.* – clown. Originates from a character in a popular 1970's children's TV show.

Patois : *n.m.* – dialect, regional language.

Pause : *n.f.* – break. Typically used on the radio to convey a "station break" (commercials).

Paver : *v.t.* – to pave.

Payer : *v.i./v.t.*- *Fr.* to pay.

- *payer la traite (à quelqu'un)* – to pay (someone's) way.

Peau : *n.f.* – *Fr.* skin.

- *peau de carriole* – carriage blanket. Typically refers to blanket found in horse-drawn carriages. *Lit.* "cart skin".

Pédaler : *v.i.* – 1. to pedal, or push with one's feet. 2. to make an effort.

Il faut que tu pédales plus vite si tu veux réussir. – You need to make more of an effort if you want to succeed.

❄ *pédaler dans le beurre* – make useless efforts *Lit.* to pedal in butter.

Peignure : *n.f.* – haircut.

Peinturer : *v.t., v.i.* – to paint.

Pelleter des nuages : *expr.* – to dream (of something unrealistic). *Lit.* to shovel clouds.

Pelure : *n.f.* – *Fr.* skin, outer layer.

❄ *enlever une pelure* – to remove one's coat. *Lit.* to take off a layer.
❄ *(s'habiller en) pelures d'oignons* – (to dress) in layers. *Lit.* "to dress in onion skins".

Pend-oreilles :*n.m.* – earring.

Penser : *v.i.* – *Fr.* to think

❄ *penser croche* – to think dirty (sexual sense).

Pentré : *n.m.* – kitchen or bathroom counter.

Pépin : *n.m* – inconvenience, problem.

Peppé : *adj.* – psyched, enthusiastic, pepped up.

Péquiste : *n.m. /f.* – supporter of the Parti Québécois.

Perdre : *v.t., v.i.* – *Fr.* to lose.

❄ *perdre sa salive* : *expr.* – to waste one's breath. *Lit.* to lose one's saliva.
❄ *perdre la track* – to go nuts, to lose one's head. *Lit.* to lose the track.

Peser : *v.t.* – to push, to depress.

   ❧ *peser sur le gaz* – to step on the gas.
   ❧ *Peser sur la suce* – to step on the gas.
   ❧ *peser sur (un bouton)* – to push on (a button).

Pétard : *adj. & n.m./fem.* – knock-out, bombshell (attractive man/woman).

Péter★ : *v.i.* – 1. to fail, breakdown. 2. *Fr.* to pass wind, to fart. 3. to exhaust, to wear out.

   Son char va péter, c'est sûr. – His car is definitely going to break down.
   Ce programme là va pèter le reste du buget. – That program is going to blow the rest of the budget.
   ❧ *Va donc péter dans les fleurs !* – Get outa here, will ya? *Lit.* Go fart in the flowers!
   ❧ *péter de la broue* – to brag about one's abilities. *Lit.* to fart suds.
   ❧ *péter la balloune* – to fail a breathalyzer (alcohol) test.
   ❧ *péter la balloune (de quelqu'un)* – to burst (someone's) bubble.
   ❧ *se péter les bretelles* – to boast, to brag *Lit.* to snap one's suspenders.
   ❧ *péter une coche* – to blow a fuse, to become furious.
   ❧ *péter au frette* – to drop dead. *Lit.* "to stop cold".
   ❧ *péter la gueule en sang* – to knock someone's teeth out. *Lit.* to explode one's mouth with blood.
   ❧ *péter plus haut que le trou★* – 1. to live above one's means. 2. to be pretentious. *Lit.* to pass wind above the hole.

Péteux (-euse) de broue : *expr.* – braggart.

Petit change : *n.m.* – loose change.

Petit coin : *n.m* – potty, bathroom. *Lit.* small corner.

Petit Crisse : *n.m. /f.* – traitor, two-faced person.

Méfies-toi, ce gars-là est un vrai petit crisse – Better watch it – that guy is really two-faced.

(aux) Petits heures : *expr.* – (to) the wee hours of the morning.

Ils se sont laissés aux petits heures. – They parted ways in the wee hours of the morning.

Piasse : *n.f.* – *sl.* buck, dollar. *Def.* piastre.

Piastre : *n.f.* – buck, dollar.

As-tu trois piastres à me passer? – Do you have three bucks you could loan me?
- *avoir des yeux rond comme des piastres* – to have eyes round like saucers.
- *changer quatre trente sous pour une piastre* – 1. to make no profit. 2. to change one thing for another of identical value. *Lit.* to change thirty cents for a quarter.
- *faire le piastre* – to make bucks, to make a lot of money.

Pic : *n.m.* – *Fr.* peak.
- *être à pic* – to be grumpy, irritable.

Pichou★★ : *n.m.* – unattractive woman.

Picosser : *v.i.* – to rummage, to forage.

Picrelle★★ : *n.f.* – prostitute, tramp.

Pied : *n.m.* – *Fr.* foot, the length of one foot.
- *être à pied* – to be in financial difficulty.
- *avoir les deux pieds dans la même bottine* – to be clumsy, unresourceful. *Lit.* "to have both feet in the same boot".

Piger : *v.t.* – to get, to grab, to take.

Pigrasser : *v.t.* – to screw around, to waste time.

Pigrasseux (-euse) : *n.m. /f.* – one who wastes time.

Pile : *n.f.* – pile.

Il laisse traîner des piles de ses affaires partout dans la maison. – He leaves piles of his stuff all over the house.

Piler : *v.t., v.i.* – 1. to peel, to scrape off. 2. to walk on, to walk over.

Attention, tu viens de piler sur mes papiers ! – Watch it, you just walked on my papers!

Piment : *n.m.* – pepper (vegetable).

❧ *piment fort* – hot pepper.

Pinch : *n.m.* – small beard encircling the mouth.

Piner : *v.i.* – to annoy, to bother, to harrass.

Il me pine là-dessus depuis deux jours. – He's been bothering me for two days about that.

Pinotte : *n.f.* – peanut.

Pinte : *n.f.* – pint.

Pipe : *n.m.* – 1. *Fr.* (smoking) pipe. 2. lie, false story.

Raconte-moi pas de pipes, je sais très bien ce qui est arrivé. – Don't lie to me, I know very well what happened.

Piquer : *v.t.* – to grab, to snatch.

❧ *piquer une crise* – to throw a fit.
❧ *piquer une jasette* – to have a chat.

Piquetage : *n.m.* – picketing.

Piqueter : *v.i.* – to picket (a place).

Pire : *adj.* – *Fr.* worst, the worst, bad.

> *au pire aller* – in the worst case.
> *c'est pas pire !* – Not bad!
> *pas si pire* – not so bad.
> *(de) pire en pire* – worse and worse.
> *pas pire, pantoute !* – Not bad, not bad at all!

Pis : *conj.* – 1. and, next. 2. "So?" 3. "What's new?" *Def.* puis.

Pis toi ? – And you?
Et pis ? – And so?

Pisse-minute : *n.f.* – someone with a frequent need to visit the bathroom.

Pissou : *n.m.* – fraidy-cat, coward.

Pitcher : *v.t.* – to throw, to pitch.

Je vais pitcher ça à la poubelle. – I'm going to throw that out.

Piton : *n.m.* – button. (*Impl.* any surface able to be pressed down).

> *être de bonne heure sur le piton* – to be up at the crack of dawn. *Lit.* to be on the button early.
> *mettre la musique dans le piton* – to play music at high volume. *Lit.* "to put music in the button".
> *(ne pas être) sur le piton* – (to not be) ready, (to not be) (*dans son assiette*)

Pitonner : *v.i.* – 1. to press a button 2. to channel surf.

Arrête de pitonner, toi ! – Stop changing channels!

Pitonneuse : *n.f.* − remote control (for a TV, etc.).

Pitou : *n.m.* − 1. pooch, dog. 2. child, kid (affectionate).

Pauvre p'tit pitou − Poor little guy.

Pitoune★★ : *n.f. & adj.* − 1. over-dressed, over-made woman. 2. floating log (from lumbering and transporting logs via river). 3. token, bingo chip.

Placer : *v.t., v.i.* − to put, to place.

❦ *placer un appel* − to place a call.

Placotage : *n.m.* − gossip, chatter.

Placoter : *v.i.* − to gossip, to chatter.

❦ *placoter sur le dos de quelqu'un* − to talk behind (someone's) back.
Ils n'arrêtaient pas de placoter sur le dos de Yannick. − They gossiped non-stop about Yannick.

Plaisant(e) : *adj.* − nice, pleasant.

Plaisir : *n.m.* − *Fr.* Fun, pleasure

❦ *plaisir coupable* − guilty pleasure

Planche : *n.f.* − *Fr.* board, plank.

❦ *à planche* − all the way, completely.
On va faire ça à planche. − We'll do it all the way.
❦ *faire de la planche (à neige)* − to snowboard.

Planification : *n.f.* − planning.

Planifier : *v.t., v.i.* − *Fr.* to plan, to schedule.

(se) Planter : *v.i.* − to fail.

Ça va planter, sûr. − It's going to fail, for certain.
Il va se planter au moment d'essayer. − He's going to fail as soon as he tries.

Plaster : *n.m.* − band-aid.

Platée : *n.f.* − plateful (of food).

Ça, c'est toute une platée ! − That's quite a plateful!

Platte : *adj.* − 1. boring, annoying 2.unfortunate.

Je la trouvais pas mal platte, son histoire. − I found his story pretty boring.
C'est platte, ça ! − That's a shame!
❦ *(une) joke platte* − a stupid joke.

Plein : *adj.* − *Fr.* full.

❦ *(en) avoir plein son casque* − to have enough. *Lit.* to have one's hat full.

Pleumer : *v.t.* − to pluck (feathers, etc).

❦ *se faire pleumer* − to get taken, to be had. *Lit.* to get plucked.

Pleurnichard : *adj.* − a cry-baby, easily crying.

Pleuvoir : *v.i.* − *Fr.* to rain

❦ *Il pleut à boire debout* − It's raining very hard. *Lit.* It's raining to drink standing up.
❦ *Il pleut des cordes* − It's raining very hard. *Lit.* It's raining cords of wood.

Pli : *n.m.* − fold, pleat.

❦ *faire un pli* − to be bothered or upset by something. Generally used in the negative: *Ça ne me fait pas un pli* − That doesn't bother me at all.

Plotte★★★ : *n.f.* – 1. slut, whore. 2. reference to female genitalia.

🌱 *avoir la plotte à terre*★★★ – to be exhausted.

🌱 *plotte à bike*★★★ – motorcycle girl.

Ploguer : *v.t.* – to plug in, to connect.

Je vais l'ploguer dans le mur. – I'll plug it in the wall.
Il est pas mal plogué dans l'industrie. – He's pretty well connected in the industry.

Pluie verglaçante : *n.f.* – freezing rain.

Plus ou moins : *expr.* – more or less. (generally implies less)

Poche : *adj.* – bad, ugly.

Son dessin était pas mal poche. – His drawing was pretty bad.

Poche : *n.f.* – male sexual organs.

Pocher : *v.t.* – to screw up, to do a bad job (on something).

Poêle : *n.m.* – stove.

Poêlon : *n.m.* – large stove.

Pogner : *v.t., v.i.* – 1. to get, to receive. 2. to grab, to trap, to catch. 3. to have (sense of possession). 4. to quarrel, to argue. 5. to be successful (esp. with the opposite sex).

J'ai pogné un rhume. – I caught a cold.
On a été pognés dans la neige pendant deux heures. – We were stuck in the snow for two hours.
C'est fou comment qu'il pogne, ce gars là – It's amazing how well that guy does with women.

🌱 *pogner son air* – to be surprised. *Lit.* to take (one's) breath.

🌱 *se faire pogner* – to get caught.

pogner une chicane – to argue, to have a dispute.

pogner le jackpot – to hit the jackpot.

pogner le Klondike – to strike it rich, to succeed.

pogner les nerfs – to become irritable, angry.

se pogner le bacon – to goof off, to do nothing

se pogner le cul – to goof off, to do nothing.

se pogner le derrière – to goof off, to do nothing

(se) Pogner : *v.i.* – to hook up, to get together (romantically).

Pogné : *adj.* – stuck.

pogné dans une combine – caught in a bad situation.
Je suis vraiment pogné là-dessus. – I'm really stuck on that point.

Poignée : *n.f.* – *Fr.* handle.

avoir une poignée dans le dos – to be gullible. *Lit.* to have a handle on one's back.

Poil : *n.f.* – *Fr.* hair.

Bibitte à poil – small animal.

s'ennerver le poil des jambes – to get upset. *Lit.* "to excite one's leg hair".

s'exciter le poil des jambes – to get upset. *Lit.* "to excite one's leg hair".

Pointe : *n.f.* – slice (of pizza or pie).

Pointer : *v.t.* – to point out, to highlight.

Il m'a pointé trois problèmes différents avec la compagnie. – He pointed out three different problems with the company.

Poli à ongles : *n.m.* – nail polish.

Police montée : *n.f.* – mounted police.

Pommes de route : *n.f. pl.* − horse droppings.

Pompette : *adj.* − drunk, intoxicated.

Popoter : *v.i.* − to cook, to prepare a meal.

Porc : *n.m.* − *Fr.* pig.

🦋 *faire des yeux de porc frais* − to be wide-eyed. *Lit.* "to have eyes like a fresh pig".

Poqué : *adj.* − 1. tired or hurt (for a person) 2. Damaged (for an object) 3. trashed, very drunk (for a person).

Poquer : *v.t.* − to damage, to dent, to ding.

Porter : *v.t.* − to carry, to bring.

Je vais te porter une pizza ce soir − I'll bring you a pizza tonight.

Possiblement : *adv.* − possibly.

Poste de TV : *n.f.* − TV station.

Poteau : *n.m.* − post, telephone pole.

🦋 *sirop de poteau* − imitation maple syrup. *Lit.* telephone pole syrup.

Potter : *v.t.* − to sink (something).

🦋 *potter un but* − to make a goal, to sink a puck (hockey)

Poucer : *v.i.* − to hitchhike, to thumb a ride.

Poudrerie : *n.f.* − wind-blown snow.

Poupoune : *n.f.* − overmade, badly-dressed woman.

Pour : *prép.* – 1. *Fr.* for. 2. according to, as for.

Pour moi, j'en ai marre. – As for me, I've had enough.
- *être pour (quelque chose)* – to be in favor of (something), to be all for (something).

Pourquoi (que) : *art., pron.* – why (the reason that). *Pourquoi* is often used directly as a pronoun:

C'est pourquoi que je suis venu. – That's why I came.

Pourriel : *n.m.* – spam (email).

Pourtant : *adv.* – nevertheless, yet.

Pousse-Pousse : *n.m.* – stoller, carriage.

Pousser : *v.t.* – *Fr.* to push

- *(être) top poussé* – too far out, to far ahead.
Ses idées sont bonnes, mais je trouve qu'elles soitent un peu trop poussés pour notre organisation – His ideas are good, but i find them a bit too far ahead for our organization.

(se) Pousser : *v.i.* – to head out, to take off.

Pousseux(-euse) : *n.m/f.* – hitchhiker.

Poutine : *n.f.* – 1. a mixture of french fries and lumps of cheese covered in gravy. 2. anything which is a mixture of various elements.

C'est toute la même poutine. – It's all the same stuff.

(se) Pouvoir : *v.i.* – to be possible, to be thinkable.

Ça ne se peut pas qu'il y soit allé ! – There's no way he could've gone!
- *Ça s'peut-tu que…* – Could it be that…

(se) Practiquer : *v.i.* – to practice.

Prélart : *n.m.* – linoleum.

❆ *mettre la musique dans le prélart* – to play music at high volume. *Lit.* "to put music in the linoleum".

Prendre : *v.t., v.i.* – *Fr.* to take.

❆ *Ça prend…* – That'll take… *Expr.* Very similar to French "*Il faut*", *Ca prend* is generally used to specify something necessary to identify a goal. Also used in the reflexive (*Ca me prends,* etc)

❆ *Ca prends deux minutes de ton temps* – It'll take just 2 minutes of your time.

❆ *Ca va te prendre une cuillère pour le manger* – You'll need a spoon to eat it.

❆ *prendre un break* – 1. to take a break. 2. to stop dating someone temporarily (romantic sense).

❆ *prendre une bouchée* – to grab a bite.

❆ *prendre une brosse* – go on a bender, to get drunk.

❆ *prendre le champs* – to drive off the road. *Lit.* to take to the fields.

❆ *prendre une chance* – to take a chance.

❆ *prendre tout son petit change* – to take all one's resources, to take great effort. *Lit.* to take all one's spare change.

❆ *prendre un coup* – to go drinking.

❆ *prendre un cours* – to take a class.

❆ *prendre une débarque* – to take a fall.

❆ *prendre une fouille* – to take a fall.

❆ *(se) prendre pour le nombril du monde* – to believe one's self to be the most important thing. *Lit.* to take one's self to be the bellybutton of the world.

❆ *prendre la passe du cochon qui tousse* – to cut corners, to take a shortcut. *Lit.* "to take the way of the coughing pig".

❆ *prendre son temps* – to take (one's) time.

❆ *prendre une touche* – to take a drag (on a cigarette, etc)

❆ *prendre ça aisé* – to take it easy.

❧ *prendre une marche* – to go for a walk.
❧ *prendre (quelque chose) en note* – to make note of something.
❧ *prendre offense* – to take offense.
❧ *prendre la part de (quelqu'un)* – to take (someone's) side.

Prérequis : *n.m., adj.* – *Fr.* requirement, prerequisite.

Présentement : *adv.* – *Fr.* currently, right now, presently.

Pressage : *n.m.* – ironing, pressing.

Presse : *n.f.* – urgency, haste.

Presser : *v.t.* – to iron, to press.

Proche : *adj.* – *Fr.* near.

❧ *passer proche de (faire quelque chose)...* – to come close to (doing something).

Prometteux(euse) : *adj.* – promising, hopeful.

Son projet n'avait pas l'air trop prometteux – His project didn't seem terribly promising.

Prix de liste : *n.m.* – list price.

Problématique : *n.f.* – problematic situation.

❧ *vider le problématique* – to get to the bottom of the problem.

(se) Promener : *v.i.* – *Fr.* to walk, to wander.

❧ *se promener en bedaine* – to go shirtless.

Prudemment : *adv.* – prudently, with caution.

Pudding chômeur : *expr.* – simple, inexpensive pudding made from flour and brown sugar. *Lit.* unemployed man's pudding.

Puck : *n.f.* – *Fr.* (hockey) puck

    niaiser avec la puck – to waste time. *Lit.* stop fooling around with the puck.

Puffeux : *n.m.* – windbag (for a person).

Pur laine : *adj.* – dyed-in-the-wool. *Lit.* "pure wool".

Lui, c'est un Québécois pur laine. – He's a dyed-in-the-wool Québécois.

Q

Quand que : *expr.* – when, whenever.

Quasiment : *adj.* – almost, *sl.* pretty much.

Quatre-par-Quatre : *n.m.*– 4-by-4, light truck.

Queneuilles : *n.f. pl.* – eyes.

Quequ' : *expr.* – ... and some. *Def.* Quelque chose. Used after numbers to imply an approximate amount:

> *Cent quequ'*– *adj.* – one hundred and some.
> *Ça m'a coûté trois cent quequ' pour réparer mon char.* – It cost me three hundred and something to fix my car.

Quequ' chose : *n.m.* – something. *Contr.* quelque chose).

Quequ' part : *adv.* – somewhere. *Contr.* quelque part).

Quéquette★ : *n.f.* – dick, penis.

> *Grosse corvette, petite quéquette !* – *Lit.* Large corvette, small dick. Saying used for a wealthy but immature person.

Quessé? : *expr.* – What is it? *Def.* Qu'est-ce que c'est?

Questa? : *expr.* – What do you have? What's wrong? *Def.* Qu'est-ce que tu as?

Quétaine : *adj.* – tasteless, bad.

> *quétaine au boutte* – completely tasteless.
> *Ces vêtements sont quétaines au boutte* – These clothes are completely tasteless

Quétainerie : *n.f.* − crap★, object in bad taste.

Sa maison est superb, mais la quétainerie qu'il a sur les murs la defait complètement. − His house is amazing, but the crap he has on the walls totally wrecks it.

Quêter : *v.i.* − to beg.

Quêteux(euse) : *n.m. /fem. & adj.* − beggar.

Quille : *n.f.* − bowling pin.

🌿 *jouer aux quilles* − to bowl, to go bowling.

Quitter : *v.i.* − to leave, to head out.

Quoi : *pron.* − *Fr.* what.

🌿 *de quoi* − something, anything.
   As-tu de quoi à faire ? − Do you have anything to do?

R

Rabais : *n.m.* – rebate, discount.

Raboudinage : *n.m.* – botched-up work.

Raboudiner : *v.t.* – to botch, to mess up.

Rackadjo : *n.m.* – breasts. *Contr.* "*Rack à jos*".

(se) Racoquiller : *v.i.* – to cower.

Ragoût de pattes : *n.m.* – traditional Québec fare made from pig's feet and beef meatballs in a rich brown stew.

Raide : *adj.* – stiff.

　⚜ *ben raide* – completely, totally. *Lit.* good and stiff.
　⚜ *fou raide* – completely nuts.
　⚜ *fucké ben raide***✶✶** – completely screwed up.
　⚜ *raide comme une barre* – stiff as a bar.

(se) Ramasser : *v.t.* – to wind up (somewhere), end up (somewhere).

Après un bout, on s'est ramassés ici. – After a bit, we ended up here.
　⚜ *se faire ramasser* – to be called on the carpet (for something), to get in trouble.

Rang : *n.m.* – 1. *Fr.* rank (in an organization). 2. country road.

　⚜ *école de rang* – country(side) school.

(se) Raplomber : *v.i.* – to find one's balance.

Raqué(e) : *adj.* – tired, exhausted, *sl.* destroyed.

Je suis trop raqué pour sortir à soir. – I'm too exhausted to go out tonight.

Raquettes : *n.f.* – (humerous) term for someone's (oversize) feet.

Ras (au) : *adj.* – near, close to.

Rase-trou : *n.m.* – short item of female clothing (such as a skirt) which is at the limit of good taste. *Lit.* scrape-hole.

Ratoureux(euse) : *n.m. /fem. & adj.* – wily, sly, crafty.

Rattrapable : *adj.* – able to be caught.

Ravage : *n.m.* – trail.

Rayé : *adj.* – scratched, scraped, dinged.

Rayer : *v.t., v.i.* – to scratch, to scrape.

Razbol : *n.m.* – bowl cut (haircut).

Recevoir : *v.t., v.i.* – *Fr.* to receive.

　🔊 *recevoir (quelque chose) sur la tomate* – be hit by something unexpected. *Lit.* to catch it on the tomato.

Réchauffé : *adj.* – 1. *Fr.* reheated 2. loaded, drunk.

Recherchist(e) : *n.m. /f.* – researcher.

Référer : *v.t., v.i.* – to refer, to pass on.

Regarder : *v.t., v.i.* – *Fr.* to look.

　🔊 *regarder bien pour...* – to look good for...
　　Ça regarde bien pour demain ! – Everything looks good for tomorrow!

Réguine : *n.f.* − Device or item that doesn't work as expected. *sl.* a lemon.

> *La tondeuse que j'ai achetée est une vraie réguine, ça fonctionne une fois sur deux.* − The lawnmower I bought is a real lemon, it works one time out of two.

Régulier : *adj.* − normal, standard.

Rejet : *n.m. /fem.* − *sl.* loser, *sl.* reject.

> *Ce gars-là est un rejet.* − That guy is a loser.

Rejoindre : *v.t.* − 1. *Fr.* to meet, to come together. 2. to contact, to a hold of, to catch (up with) someone.

> *Tu peux le rejoindre chez lui.* − You can catch him at home.

Remorqueuse : *n.f.* − tow-truck.

Remplissage : *n.m.* − refill.

> *remplissage gratuit* − free refill.

Renforcir : *v.t.* − to strengthen.

Renipper : *v.t.* − to fix up, to repair.

> *Mon chum a renippé son char l'été dernier* − My boyfriend fixed up his car last summer.

Rentrer : *v.i.* − *Fr.* to re-enter (a house, or other structure), to go home

> *(se) faire rentrer dedan*s − 1. to be hit (by a vehicle or object) 2. to be scolded or otherwise verbally berated

Revirer : *v.i.* − to swing around, to turn around.

> *(se) revirer sur un trente sou* − to turn on a dime.

Renvoyer : *v.t.* – 1. to send back, to send away. 2. to vomit, to throw up.

> *J'ai renvoyé le colis le lendemain.* – I sent the package back the next morning.
>
> ❧ *se faire renvoyer* – 1. to be sent away. 2. to lose one's job.

Reseaurage : *n.m.* – networking, social interaction.

Résident(e) : *n.m. /fem.* – *Fr.* resident, inhabitant.

Ressorer : *v.t. /v.i.* – to spin.

Resoudre : *v.i.* – to arrive uninvited.

Respirer : *v.i.* – *Fr.* to breathe.

> ❧ *respirer par le nez* – to calm down. *Lit.* "to breathe through the nose".

Restable : *adj.* – livable, decent. *Lit.* stayable.

> *On a quitté assez vite puisque le bar n'était pas très restable.* – We left pretty quickly since the bar wasn't very decent.

Rester : *v.i.* – 1. *Fr.* to stay. 2. to live, to abide in.

> *On reste à Jonquière en ce moment.* – We're living in Jonquière at the moment.
>
> ❧ *rester assis sur son steak* – to sit on one's butt, to not do anything.

Restituer : *v.t., v.i.* – to vomit.

Retontir : *v.i.* – to arrive uninvited.

> *Georges a tendance à retontir à l'heure du souper.* – George tends to arrive uninvited around dinnertime.

Retourner : *v.t., v.i.* − *Fr.* to return, to revisit.

 ❧ *retourner un appel (téléphonique)*− to call back, to return someone's (telephone) call.

Retracer : *v.t.* − to find again, to rediscover.

On n'a jamais pu retracer le même chemin pour retourner. − We were never able to find the way back there.

Revenir : *v.i.* − *Fr.* to return, to come back.

 ❧ *revenir à (ses) moutons* − to come back to the subject at hand. *Lit.* to get back to one's sheep.

Revirer : *v.i.* − to swing around, to turn around, to reverse course.

Je vais revirer vers Montréal. − I'm going to turn back towards Montréal.

 ❧ *(se) revirer sur un trente sou* − to turn on a dime.

Revirer : *v.i.* − to turn around, to reverse course.

Je vais revirer vers Montréal. − I'm going to turn back towards Montréal.

Revoler : *v.t.* − to fly apart, to scatter.

Ricaneux(euse) : *n.m./fem. & adj.* − mocking, scoffing.

Rider : *v.t.* − to push (someone) hard, to ride someone.

Rien : *pron.* − *Fr.* nothing.

 ❧ *Il n'y a rien là.* − It's nothing.

Rince-bouche : *n.m.* − mouth-wash.

Rincer : *v.t.* − *Fr.* to rinse.

 ❧ *se rincer le bec* − to have a drink. *Lit.* To rinse one's beak.

Rire : *v.i.* – *Fr.* to laugh

   ❦ *rire comme un défonçé* – to die laughing.

Robine : *n.f.* – *sl.* rotgut, bad-quality alcohol.

Robineux(euse) : *n.m.* /*fem.* – drunkard, bum.

Rond(e) : *adj.* – *Fr.* round

   ❦ *être rond comme une bine* – to be completely sloshed (drunk). *Lit.* "to be as round as a bean".

Rondelette : *adj.* – chubby, overweight (used for a girl or woman).

Rondouillette : *n.f.* – chubby, overweight woman

Roteux : *n.m.* – hot dog.

Rôties : *n.m. pl.* – toast.

Rouge : *n.m.* – *Fr.* red.

   ❦ *voir rouge* – to see red (be angry).

   ❦ *être dans le rouge* – to be in the red, to be in financial difficulty.

Rouler : *v.t.* – *Fr.* to roll

   ❦ *rouler sa bosse* – to show one's wisdom. *Lit.* "to roll one's bump".

Rouleuse : *n.f.* – hand-rolled cigarette.

Roulotte : *n.f.* – trailer, camper.

   ❦ *roulotte à patates* – mobile food stand selling french fries.

Route pavée : *n.f.* – paved road.

Roux : *n.m.* – russet, brownish-red. Popular women's hair color.

Ruban (adhésif) : *n.m.* – (adhesive) tape.

Rubber : *n.m.* – 1. tire. 2. Boot(s). 3. Condom.

Ruine-babines : *n.f.* – harmonica.

Runnings : *n.m.pl.* – running shoes.

Rushant(e) : *adj.* – hurried, rushing, stressful.
Mon travail était rushant. – My job was stressfull.

Rusher : *v.i.* – to be in a rush.

S

Sa : *expr.* − on the. *Contr. "sur la".*

Sabler : *v.t.* − to sand (using sandpaper).

Sacoche : *n.f.* − handbag, pocketbook.

⚜ *sacoche d'école* − school bag.

Sacrament! : *expr.* − By all that's holy!

Sacrant : *adj.* − annoying, aggravating.

⚜ *au plus sacrant* − as quickly as possible.

Sacre : *n.m.* − oath, blasphemy.

Sacrer : *v.i.* − 1. to swear, to curse. 2. to put or place something in a careless manner. 3. not to care.

Il a descendu tous les saints du ciel tant y a sacré. − He swore so much that he brought all the saints down from the heavens.
J'ai sacré ta jupe sur le comptoir. − I threw your dress on the counter.
Je m'en sacre si tu veux pas y aller! − I don't give a damn if you don't want to go!
⚜ *se faire sacrer à la porte* − to be thrown out (of a job).
⚜ *sacrer son camp** − to leave, to head out.
⚜ *sacrer la paix* − to leave (someone) alone.
⚜ *sacrer (quelqu'un) dehors* − to throw (someone) out.
Pourrais-tu me sacrer la paix, s'il te plaît? − Could you give me a little peace, please?

Salle de montre : *n.f* − showroom.

Sans-dessein : *adj. & n.m./fem.* − clueless, thoughtless (person).

Saper : *v.i.* – to chew with one's mouth open.

Sapin : *n.m.* – *Fr.* fir tree.

> ❈ *(se faire) passer un sapin* – to be had, to get a bad deal. *Lit.* to be handed a fir tree.

Sarrau : *n.m.* – medical jacket.

(se) Saucer : *v.t.* – to dip onseself (gradually) in water, to get wet

Saucette : *n.f.* – 1. brief visit. 2. a dip (in a pool, etc.).

> ❈ *faire une saucette* – to go for a dip.
> *On va faire une saucette dans la piscine.* – We're going to take a dip in the pool.

Saut : *n.m.* – jump, start.

> ❈ *faire un saut* – to jump, to start.
> *J'ai fait un saut quand il a ouvert la porte.* – I jumped when he opened the door.

Sauté : *adj.* – 1. incredible, unbelievable, mind-blowing, nuts. 2. crazy, insane (for a person). *Lit.* jumped.

> *J'ai vu ce film hier, c'est complètement sauté !* – I saw that film yesterday – it was just mind-blowing.

Sauter : *v.t.* – *Fr.* to jump, to leap.

> ❈ *sauter la clôture* – to cheat on one's spouse. *Lit.* "to jump the gate".
> ❈ *sauter une coche* – to blow a fuse, to become furious.
> ❈ *sauter un gasket* – to blow a gasket, to become furious.

Sauver : *v.t.* – to save, to conserve.

(se) Sauver : *v.i.* – *Fr.* to escape, to leave in a hurry.

> *Il va se sauver du party bientôt.* – He's going to leave the party soon.

Scalper : *v.t.* – to scalp tickets.

Schnoute★ : *n.f.* – shit.

🔆 *mange de la schnoute !* – eat shit!

Scie à chaîne : *n.f.* – chainsaw.

Scorer : *v.t.* – 1. to score (a goal). 2. *sl.* to score (sexual sense).

Scrammer : *v.i.* – to scram, to leave quickly.

Scrappe : *n.f.* – junk.

Mon char, c'est de la scrappe. – My car is a heap.

🔆 *cour à scrap*- junkyard.

Scrapper : *v.t.* – 1. to throw out, to trash (something) 2. to crash (while skiing, etc)

J'ai scrappé mon vélo l'autre jour. – I trashed my bike the other day.

Scratcher : *v.t.* – to scratch (something).

S'cuze! : *expr.* – Excuse me! *Def.* Excuse-moi !

🔆 *S'cuzez la !* – Thank you very much! In traditional Québec music, often heard at the end of a song.

Sécheuse : *n.f.* – drying machine, dryer.

Séchoir : *n.m.* – hair-dryer.

Secousse : *n.f.* – a while, a period of time.

Ça fait une secousse que je n'y suis pas allé. – It's been a while since I've been there.

Seineux(euse) : *n.m. /fem.* – *sl.* busy-body.

Sent-bon : *n.m.* − perfume, eau-de-toilette.

Senteux(euse) : *adj. & n.m./fem.* − Curious, nosy, tactless (person).

Sentir : *v.i.*− 1.*Fr.* to feel. 2. to smell

❧ *se sentir (tout) croche* − to feel (really) bad, to be unhappy.
❧ *sentir le swing* − to smell of sweat.
❧ *sentir l'yâble* − to smell awful. *Lit.* "to smell like the devil"

Séparatiste : *n.m./fem., adj.*− one who supports the political separation of Québec from Canada.

Séraphin : *n.m.* − miser.

Serre-la-piastre : *n.m/f.* − Miser, greedy person. *Lit.* "Coin-hugger"

Serrer : *v.t.* − 1. *Fr.* to squeeze, to tighten. 2. to put away.

Veux-tu me serrer ça − Would you please put that away for me?
❧ *(se) serrer la babiche* − to tighten one's belt, to cut down

Serviable : *adj.* − usable, workable.

Set carré : *n.m.* − square dance.

Shafter : *v.i./v.t.* − to give (someone) the shaft.to screw over.

Shaker : *v.i.* − to tremble, to shake (from fright, etc.)

Sharp : *adj.* − 1. smart (for a person) 2. nice, appealing, cool, great.

Shiner : *v.t.* − to shine.

❧ *shiner (ses) souliers* − to shine (one's) shoes.

Shipper : *v.t.* − to send, to ship.

Je vais lui shipper la boîte demain. − I'll ship him the box tomorrow.

Shirer : *v.i.* − 1. to shear, to twist sideways. 2. to slide.

Mon char a shiré sur la glace. − My car slid on the ice.

Shooter : *v.t., v.i.* − 1. to send, transmit. 2. to shoot.

Shoote-moi le fichier et je l'imprime. − Shoot me over the file, and I'll print it out for you.

Siffleux : *n.m.* − marmot

Signaler : *v.t.* − 1. to indicate (especially, by depressing a button on a phone) 2. to signal

Pour rejoindre le téléphoniste, signalez le 0. − To reach an operator, press 0.

Simonaque : *expr.* − Dammit!

Sirop d'érable : *n.m.* − maple syrup.

Sirop de poteau : *expr.* − imitation maple syrup. *Lit.* telephone pole syrup.

Slaquer : *v.i.* − *sl.* to goof off, to relax.

Sloune : *n.f.* − (beach) sandal.

Smatte : *adj.* − 1. pleasant, nice 2. show-off

🍁 *(un) beau smatte* − one who disappoints by his behavior.
🍁 *faire son smatte* − to show off.

Soda à pâte : *n.f* − bicarbonate of soda.

Soignable : *adj.* − able to be healed.

Soir : *n.m.* − *Fr.* evening

🍁 *Drette à soir* − As of this evening

Son chien est mort : *expr.* – to be done-in, to be finished. *Lit.* His dog is dead.

Songé(e) : *adj.* – wise, insightful, thought-through.

> *Il n'est pas le gars le plus songé du monde.* – He's not the most brilliant guy in the world.

Sortir : *v.i.* – *Fr.* to leave, to depart.

> ✿ *sortir du bois* – to make it out of the woods, to escape trouble.
> ✿ *sortir du garde-robe* – to come out of the closet, to reveal one's homosexuality.
> *Je ne peux pas m'en sortir encore.* – I can't get out of it yet.

Sou : *n.m.* – cent, penny.

> *Est-ce que t'as un vingt-cinq sous ?* – Do you have a quarter?
> ✿ *(se) revirer sur un trente sou* – to turn on a dime.

Soubassement : *n.m.* – (sub)basement.

Soue : *n.f.* – sty

> ✿ *soue à cochons* – pigsty.
> ✿ *ferme ta soue !* – shut your trap! *Lit.* shut your sty!

Souffler : *v.t.* – to inflate, to blow up.

> *Je vais souffler les ballons pour les enfants.* – I'm going to blow up the balloons for the kids.
> ✿ *souffler dans la balloune.* – to take a breathalyzer test. *Lit.* to blow in the balloon.

Souffleuse : *n.f.* – 1. snowblower. 2 snow plow.

Souliers : *n.m., pl.* – (low-cut) shoes.

Soule : *adj.* − *Fr.* drunk.

  ❧ *soule comme une botte* − completely wasted, inebriated. *Lit.* as drunk as a boot.

Soûlon(ne) : *adj. & n.m. /fem.* − drunk, intoxicated.

Soupe : *n.f.* − *Fr.* soup.

  ❧ *voir (quelqu'un) dans (ma) soupe* − to be caught up with someone, to be head-over-heels for someone. *Lit.* "to see (someone) in (my) soup."

Soupane : *n.f.* − oatmeal.

Souper : *n.m.* − dinner, evening meal.

  ❧ *souper communautaire* − pot-luck dinner.

Sous : *adv.* − *Fr.* below, under.

  Quarante degrés sous zéro − Forty degrees below zero.

  ❧ *sous l'impression (que)* − under the impression (that).

Sous-contracteur : *n.m.* − sub-contractor.

Sous-marin : *n.m.* − submarine (sandwich).

Sous-plat : *n.m.* − hotplate.

Souverainist(e) : *n.m. /fem., adj.* − One who supports the political separation of Québec from Canada.

Spinner : *v.t.* − to spin (around).

Splitter : *v.t.* − to split, to divide.

  Pour la facture, veux-tu la splitter? − As for the check, shall we split it?

Spotter : *v.t.* – to notice, to spot.

On s'est fait spotter tout de suite. – We were noticed right away.

Squeegee : *n.m./fem.* – Adolescent taken to cleaning windshields at stoplights to earn money.

Squeezer : *v.t., v.i.* – to squeeze, to fit.

Stacose (que) : *expr.* – because, since. *Def.* C'est à cause (que).

Staller : *v.i., v.t.* – to stall, to deliberately delay.

Son projet a pas mal stallé. – His project has pretty much stalled.

Stationner : *v.i., v.t.* – to park (a car).

Stationnement : *n.m.* – parking lot.

Steak : *n.m.* – *Fr.* steak, beef.

  être assis sur son steak – 1. to sit on one's butt, to be lazy. 2. to be in a comfortable financial position. *Lit.* to be seated upon (one's) steak.

Stepper : *v.i.* – to start or jump (from surprise).

Quand il m'a parlé, ça m'a tellement surpris que j'ai steppé. – When he spoke to me, it surprised me so much that I started.

Stoné : *adj.* – stoned (on drugs).

Straight : *adj.* – conservative, law-abiding, up-front.

S'tu… : *expr.* – Is it that… *Def.* Est-ce que c'est…

Stock : *n.m.* – stuff. Effectively, the plural form of "*stuff*" (below).

Stuff : *n.m.* – stuff. Different from English, used only to refer to a single object which is of uncountable quality – such as a medicinal cream, a volume of liquid, a powder, etc.

> *T'es-tu coupé ? J'ai du stuff à mettre dessus, si tu veux.* – Did you cut yourself? I have some stuff to put on that, if you want.
> *As-tu ajouté dans le punch le stuff que t'as amené ?* – Did you add that stuff you brought to the punch?

Suce : *n.f.* – 1. sucker (for an infant). 2. accelerator (in a car).

> ❧ *pèser sur la suce* – to step on the gas.

Suce-la-cenne : *n.m./f.* – Miser, greedy person. *Lit.* "Coin-sucker"

Sucette : *n.f.* – hickey, red mark left on the skin from a kiss.

Suçon : *n.m.* – lollipop.

Sucrer : *v.t., v.i.* – *Fr.* to sugar, to sweeten.

> ❧ *se sucrer le bec* – to eat, particularly sweets.

Suisse : *n.m.* – squirrel.

Suiveux : *adj. & n.m./fem.* – follower (not a leader)

Supporter : *v.t.* – 1. *Fr.* to put up with. 2. to encourage, to support.

Supposé : *adj.* – supposed (to).

> ❧ *être supposé de…* – to be supposed to…
> *Elle est supposée y aller.* – She's supposed to go (there).

Supposément : *adv.* – supposedly.

Sur : *art.* – *Fr.* on.

> ❧ *être sur le bord de…* – to be about to.

Surprendre : *v.t., v.i.* – to surprise.

Ça me surprend un peu. – That surprises me a bit.

Swell : *adj* – well-dressed, chic.

Swing la bacaisse dans l'fond de la boîte à bois : *expr.* – Traditional square-dancing expression, used to poke fun at more portly dancing women. *Lit.* "Swing your backside at the bottom of the buffet (table)".

Swinger : *v.i.* – to party, to dance, to have a good time.

Ça va swinger ce soir. – It's gonna be a blast this evening!
Ça swingue en grand – to work beautifully.

Switcher : *v.t., v.i.* – to change, to switch.

Système de son : *expr.* – sound system, stereo.

T

Tabagie : *n.f.* – newspaper stand.

Tabarnac : *expl.* – Goddamn! *Lit.* the tabernacle, the place where the Eucharist is kept in a Roman Catholic church.

Table à café : *n.f.* – coffee table.

Table d'hôte : *n.m.* – restaurant's daily special, usually including an appetizer, a main dish, and dessert/coffee. *Lit.* host's table.

Tablette : *adj.* – room-temperature.

Cette bière est pas mal tablette! – This beer is pretty much room temperature!

Taboire : *expl.* – Hell! (softer form of *Tabarnac*).

C'est une taboire de belle opportunité. – It's one hell of a great opportunity.

Tag ou bitche? : *expr.* – heads or tails?

T'à l'heure : *expr.* – 1. earlier. 2. later. *Def.* tout à l'heure.

Tannant(e) : *adj.* – boring, annoying.

L'histoire était un peu tannante. – The story was a bit boring.

Tanné (de) : *adj.* – tired of, fed up, bored with (something/someone).

Viens-t'en, chérie, je suis tanné. – C'mon, sweetie, I'm tired of this...

Tanner : *v.t.* – to bore, to make tired of (something).

Tant que... : *Fr.* as for...

⚜ *tant qu'à y être* – insofar as that may be (the case).

Tantôt : *adv.* – 1. before. 2. soon, afterwards. Can be used in either sense, depending on the context or the tense of the verb used.

À tantot ! – See you later!
Je t'appelle tantôt. – I'll call you later.
Tantôt tu m'avais dit que non. – Earlier, you (had) told me no.

Taoin : *n.m.* – simpleton, imbecile.

Tapette : *n.m.* – effeminate man.

Taper : *v.t.* – *Fr.* to tap, to smack, to hit.

taper sur les nerfs – to exasperate, to annoy. *Lit.* to hit on one's nerves.
Il arrêtait pas de me taper sur les nerfs. – He wouldn't stop annoying me.

se taper une broue – to have a beer.

Tapis : *n.m.* – *Fr.* carpet, rug.

mettre la musique dans le tapis – to play music at high volume. *Lit.* "to put music in the carpet".

Taponnage : *n.m.* – hesitation, dallying.

Taponner : *v.i.* – to dally, to beat around the bush.

Arrête de taponner et donne-moi la réponse ! – Stop dallying and give me the answer!

Taponneux(euse) : *n.m./fem., adj.* – one who hesitates or dallies.

Tarla : *n.m.* – idiot, fool.

Tas : *n.m.* – a bunch, a cluster (of something)

Tata : *n.m./fem. & adj.* – 1. goodbye wave. 2. imbecile, simpleton.

faire tata – to wave goodbye.

Tataouinage : *n.m.* − indecision, hesitation.

Tataouiner : *v.i.* − to fool around, to waste time (on unimportant things).

Tax de Bienvenue : *n.m.* − welcome tax. Typically, taxes owed to the Québec Government upon purchase of a new house or condominium.

Teigne : *n.m. /fem.* − pestering or harrassing person.

Téléroman : *n.m.* − TV series, such as a sitcom or soap opera.

Téléphone : *n.m.* − 1. *Fr.* telephone. 2. telephone call.

J'ai eu un téléphone de lui hier. − I got a call from him yesterday.

Tempête de neige : *n.f.* − snowstorm.

Temps : *n.m.* − *Fr.* time.

　❦　*à temps* − in time.
　❦　*avoir le temps dans sa poche* − to take one's time, to go slowly. *Lit.* to have the time in one's pocket.
　❦　*faire du temps* − to do time (in prison).
　❦　*Temps des sucres* − the period (typically March through April) within which maple syrup is being harvested, and sugar shacks (Cabanes à sucre) are open.
　　Ne t'inquiète pas, il va arriver à temps. − Don't worry, he'll arrive on time.

Tends : *expr.* − *Def.* Attends.

Tends minute ! − Wait a sec!

Tenir : *v.t.* – *Fr.* to hold.

> *tenir à (quelqu'un)* – to care about someone.
> *tenir le gros bout du bâton* – to have the advantage *Lit.* to hold the big end of the stick).

Je tiens beaucoup à toi – I care about you a lot.

Tenter : *v.i.* – 1. *Fr.* to try, to attempt. 2. to tempt, to interest.

J'ai tenté de le faire tantôt. – I tried to do it earlier.
Est-ce que ça te tente de venir avec nous ? – Are you interested in coming with us?

Terre : *n.f.* – *Fr.* earth

> *à terre* – exhausted, finished, dead.

La batterie dans ma voiture est complètement à terre – My car battery is completely dead.

> *(avec les) culottes à terre* – (with one's) pants down.
> *avoir la face à terre* – to be annoyed, to be vexed.
> *avoir la langue à terre* – 1. to be exhausted. 2. to be very hungry. *Lit.* "to have (one's) tongue on the ground".

Tête : *n.f.* – *Fr.* head.

> *avoir la tête à Papineau* – to be very intelligent.
> *tête de rubber* – numskull, dunce. *Lit.* rubber head.

Téter : *v.i.* – to hesitate.

Téteux(euse) : *n.m./fem. & adj.* – 1. *sl.* boot-licker, brown-noser. 2. hesitant person.

'ti : *Def.* – *Fr.* petit (small).

Je prendrais bien un 'ti café – I'll take a small coffee.

Tieindre : *v.t., v.i.* – to hold.

Tiguidou : *expr.* – *sl.* okey-dokey.

Tinker : *v.t.* – 1. to fail, *sl.* to tank, *sl.* to go belly-up. 2. to fill up (a tank), *Ex.* that of a car.

Son projet va sûrement tinker. – His project is definitely going to fail.

Je vais aller tinker d'abord. – I'm going to fill up my car first.

Tipper : *v.t.* – to tip (someone).

Tire (d'érable) : *n.m.* – hot maple sirop, spread onto snow to cool, and wrapped around a stick to form a lollipop. A typical dessert made at a *Cabane à Sucre.*

Tirer : *v.t.* – *Fr.* to pull.

- *tirer le diable par la queue* – to be very poor. *Lit.* to pull the devil by the tail.
- *(se) tirer la pipe* – to pull (someone's) leg. *Lit.* to pull the pipe.
- *(se) tirer une bûche* – to join in (a conversation, etc). *Lit.* to pull up a log.

Tizoune : *n.m./fem.* – dunce.

Toaste dorée : *n.m.* – french toast.

Toastes : *n.m.* – toast.

- *aller aux toasts* – to score, to hit a goal.

Tomber : *v.i.* – *Fr.* to fall.

- *tomber en amour* – to fall in love.
- *tomber sur les nerfs* – to exasperate, to annoy. *Lit.* to hit on one's nerves.

  Il arrêtait pas de me tomber sur les nerfs. – He wouldn't stop annoying me.

Toasté : *adj.* – 1. toasted, grilled; 2. drunk.

 toasté des deux bords. – completely sloshed, very drunk. *Lit.* toasted on both sides.

Toaster : *v.t.* – 1. to toast 2. to overuse, to burn out.

Tôle : *adj.* – broke, penniless.

Tolérer : *v.i.* – to tolerate, to put up with someone or something.

Tomate : *n.f.* – *Fr.* tomato

 recevoir (quelque chose) sur la tomate – be hit by something unexpected *sim.* "to catch it on the chin". *Lit.* to catch it on the tomato.

Tomber : *v.i.* – *Fr.* to fall.

 tomber en amour – to fall in love.
 tomber en compote – to fall to pieces.
 tomber sur les nerfs – to exasperate, to annoy. *Lit.* to hit on one's nerves.
 Il arrêtait pas de me tomber sur les nerfs. – He wouldn't stop annoying me.

Toppe : *n.f.* – cigarette.

Toquant(e) : *adj.* – heavy, filling (for food).

 La bouffe était bonne et assez toquante ! – The food was great, and pretty filling.

Torcher : *v.i.* – 1. to move rapidly. 2. to not care (*s'en torcher**). 3. to clean in a rough manner.

 Y torche, ton char ! – Hey, your car really moves!
 Je m'en torche s'il vient ou non. – I don't give a damn if he comes along or not.

Torchon : *n.m.* – rag.

   A chaque guenille son torchon – To every girl her guy. *Lit.* to each cloth its rag.

Tordre : *v.t.* – *Fr.* to twist

   tordre le bras (de quelqu'un) – to twist (someone's) arm, to insist.

Torrieux : *expl.* – Damn!

Torvis : *expl.* – Damn!

Toton : *n.m./fem., adj.* – 1. idiot, fool. 2. (*n.m. pl.*) *boobs, breasts.*

Touche : *n.f.* – drag, hit (of a cigarette, etc).

   prendre une touche – to take a drag.

Toué : *contr.* – all the… *Def.* "*tous les*".

   en toué cas – in all cases…

Touffe★★ : *n.f.* – 1. woman of questionable reputation. 2. woman's genital hair.

Toffer : *v.t.* – to put up with (something), to tough (something) out.

   Ça fait mal, mais je peux le tougher. – It hurts, but I can take it.

Toune : *n.f.* – Tune, melody.

Tourlou : *expr.* – Toodleoo. Used as "goodbye".

Tourmaline★★ : *n.f.* – 1. woman's hat, usually of large proportions. 2. cow dung.

Tourner : *v.i.* – *Fr.* to turn.

   tourner dans le beurre – to go nowhere. *Lit.* "to turn in butter

Tourtière : *n.f.* − meat pie.

Tout(e) : *n.m.* − *Fr.* all, everything.

    tout le kit − everything, the whole bit.

    tout le long − the entire time.
      *On sort ensemble, on se voit deux, trois fois par semaine, tout le
      kit.* − Yep, we're going out together − we see each other two
      three times a week, the whole bit.

Tout croche : *adj., adv.* − 1. bad, badly. 2. dirty, distasteful.

    Tu parles espagnol tout croche. − You speak Spanish badly.

Toutoune : *n.f.*- roly-poly woman.

TPS : *n.m.* − Federal sales tax.

Track : *n.m.* − (train) track

    être à coté de la track − to be in error, to make a mistake. *Lit.* to
    be next to the (train) track.

    perdre la track − to go nuts, to lose one's head. *Lit.* to lose the
    track.

Traduisible : *adj.* − able to be translated.

Traîne sauvage : *n.m.* − sled, toboggan.

Traîner : *v.t., v.i.* − *Fr.* to drag, to haul, to tow.

    se traîner les pieds − to drag one's feet, to take one's time.

Traîneux(euse) : *n.m./fem. & adj.* − 1. slow person. 2. someone who
constantly makes a mess (leaving a trail of disorder).

Trâlée : *n.f.* − procession, large quantity of things or people.

    Elle est arrivée à l'école avec sa trâlée d'étudiants. − She came to the
school with her procession of students.

Tranquillement (pas vite) : *expr.* − slowly, gently.

Trappe : *n.f.* − trap, mouth, yap.

Ferme donc ta trappe ! − Shut your mouth, already!

Traversier : *n.m.* − ferry, water shuttle.

Trente-sous : *n.m.* − quarter, 25 cent piece. *Lit.* thirty cents.

Trimer : *v.t.* − to trim, to cut.

Trippant(e) : *adj.* − impressive, amazing, exciting.

Tripper : *v.t.* − 1. *sl.* to dig something, to find something cool, to really like something. 2. to have a crush on (someone).

Je trippe sur son projet ! − I really dig his project!

Trippeux(-euse) : *n.m/f & adj* − (one who) really enjoys (something).

Trognon : *n.m.* − troll.

Trôler : *v.i., v.t.* − to troll, to try and catch someone or something.

Il a pas arrêté de trôler pour un date toute la soirée. − He kept looking for a date the entire evening.

Trône : *n.m.* − throne, toilet.

  ❧ *être sur le trône* − to be on the throne.

Trou : *n.m.* − 1. *Fr.* hole. 2. *sl.* a dive, a less-than-nice place. 3. *trou de cul*∗∗ − *Fr.* asshole.

Va pas à ce bar-là, c'est un trou. − Don't go to that bar, it's a dive.

  ❧ *avoir le trou de cul en dessous du bras* − *Lit.* to be exhausted. To have one's asshole under the arm.

  ❧ *boire comme un trou* − to drink like a fish. *Lit.* to drink like a hole.

❧ *être dans le trou* – to be in trouble. *Lit.* to be in a hole.

❧ *péter plus haut que le trou*★★ – to be a snob. *Lit.* to fart above the hole.

Trou de beigne : *n.m.* – doughnut hole.

Trouble : *n.m.* – trouble, problem.

❧ *Il n'y a pas de trouble !* – No problem!

T'sais : *expr.* – Y'know. *Contr.* tu sais.

Truster : *v.t.* – to have confidence in, to trust.

Tuile : *n.f.* – tile.

Tuque : *n.f.* – winter hat.

❧ *attacher (sa) tuque (avec de la broche)* – To hang on to your hat, to be ready for something
Attache ta tuque, on va aller skiier sur la piste difficile après ! – Hang onto your hat, we're going to ski down the difficiult slope next!

Turluter : *v.t., v.i.* – to hum, to sing.

Toutoune : *n.f. & adj.* – small overweight woman.

Tuyeau : *n.m.* – 1. *Fr.* pipe. 2. Connection (between people), an "in".

Twit : *n.m./fem., adj.* – idiot, fool, twit.

❧ *C'est un beau twit !* – He's a complete idiot!

U, V

Ustensiles : *n.m. pl. – Fr.* utensils, cutlery.

Vacances de le construction : *n.m.pl.* – yearly holiday for most of the building construction business in Québec – typically the 2nd half of July.

Vache : *n.m. – Fr.* cow.

   Le diable est aux vaches – Used to describe a chaotic situation. *Lit.* "the devil is in the cows".

Vacher : *v.i.* – to laze around, to loaf

Vaisseau : *n.m.* – (big) cook pot.

Valise : *n.m.* – 1. *Fr.* suitcase. 2. trunk (of a car).

Valeur : *n.f. – Fr.* value.

   être d'valeur – to be a shame, to be unfortunate. *C'est d'valeur, mais on est déjà pris.* – Unfortunately, we're already busy.

Varger : *v.t.* – to beat, to strike with force.

   Il était tellement fâché qu'il a vargé dans le mur. – He was so angry that he hit the wall.
   C'est pas vargeux – It's not very strong, it's not brilliant.

Vatendon : *expr.* – "Go on then!" "You're kidding me!" (*Def.* Va t'en donc.)

Vedg : *adj.* – vegged-out, relaxed, at ease.

   Man, je suis complètement veg. – Man, I'm totally vegged out.

Vedger : *v.i.* – to vege out, laze about, to loaf.

Je n'ai rien fait tout la journée – j'ai vedgé sur le divan – I didn't to anything all day – just vegged out on the sofa.

Veillée : *n.f.* – evening.

❧ *veillée au corps* – wake.

Veiller : *v.i.* – to spend the evening, usually at someone's house.

On va veiller chez lui ce soir. – We're spending the evening at his place.

Veilleux(euse) : *n.m./fem. + adj.* – one who likes to go to bed very late.

Vente : *n.f.* – *Fr.* sale.

❧ *vente de feu* – fire-sale
❧ *vente de garage* – garage sale.
❧ *vente de trottoir* – sidewalk sale

Venter : *v.i.* – to be windy.

Venteux : *adj.* – windy.

Ventiler : *v.i.* – 1. to air out. 2. *sl.* blow off steam, to vent (one's anger).

Versatile : *adj.* – multi-talented, skilled in several fields.

Veston : *n.m.* – suit jacket.

Viande hachée : *n.f.* – hamburger meat.

Viarge★★ : *expl.* – Goddamit! *Lit.* Virgin – allusion to the Virgin Mary.

Vidanges : *n.f. pl.* – garbage, trash.

Vidangeur : *n.m.* – garbage man.

Vider : *v.t, v.i.* – *Fr.* to empty

  ❧ *vider le problematique* – to get to the bottom of the problem.

Vignenne : *n.m/f & adj* – (one who is a) rascal, rebel.

Virailler : *v.i.* – 1. to circle, to circumnavigate. 2. to toss and turn in bed.

  On a viraillé dans le voisinage pendant une demi-heure, mais on n'a pas pu trouver sa maison. – We circled the neighborhood for half an hour, but couldn't find his house.

Virer : *v.i.* – to turn.

  ❧ *aller virer à...* – to head out to...
  ❧ *virer de bord* – to turn around.
  ❧ *virer fou* – *sl.* to go nuts, to go out of one's mind.
  ❧ *virer sur le top* – to become the best.

Viser : *v.t., v.i.* – *Fr.* to forsee, to predict.

  Je vise que ça pourrait prendre une bonne semaine. – I'd say it could take a good week.

Visionner : *v.t.* – to watch. (a film, a movie, etc)

Visite : *n.f.* – visitors. Generally used in the partitive (*de la visite*), when referring to houseguests.

  ❧ *avoir de la visite* – to have house guests/company.

Vitement : *adv.* – quickly.

Voir : *v.t., v.i.* – *Fr.* to see.

  ❧ *voir (quelqu'un) dans (ma) soupe* – to be caught up with someone, to be head-over-heels for someone. *Lit.* "to see (someone) in (my) soup."

Votation : *n.f.* − voting.

Vous autres : *pron.* − *sl.* y'all, you all.

Voûte : *n.f.* − vault, safe-box.

Voyage : *n.m.* − trip, voyage.

> *avoir son voyage* − to have had enough, to be fed up.
> *C'est la denière fois que je passerais une soirée chez eux − j'ai mon voyage !* − That's the last time I'll spend the evening at their place − I've had enough!

Voyons donc ! : *expr.* − "C'mon!" "I don't believe it!" *Lit.* Let's see then.

> *Voyons donc ! Je veux te voir !* − C'mon! I want to see you!

Vues : *n.f. pl.* − movies.

> *aller aux vues* − to go to the movies.
> *écouter une vue* − to watch a movie.

W

Wack : *n.m.* – shout, yell.

 lâcher un wack – to let out a yell.

Watcher : *v.t.* – to oversee. *sl.* to keep an eye on (something/someone).

Wo ! (là) : *expr.* – "Stop!", "That's enough!"

X, Y

Y'a ça : *expr.* − there is that (i.e. that is true). *Contr.* "*Il y a ça*"

Y'a rien là : *expr.* − it's unimportant, there's no issue. *Contr.* "*Il n'y a rien là*".

Yâble : *n.m.* − devil. (*Def. Diable*).

 sentir l'yâble − to smell awful. *Lit.* "To smell like the devil".

Yeule : *n.f.* − mouth (*Def.* gueule).

Yeux : *n.m. pl.* − *Fr.* eyes.

 avoir des yeux (tout) croches − to have squinty eyes.
 avoir des yeux dans la graisse de bines − to be glassy-eyed. *Lit.* "to have one's eyes in the bean grease".
 avoir les deux yeux dans le même trou − to be exhausted, i.e. to be staring at a point in space. *Lit.* "to have both one's eyes in the same hole".
 coûter les yeux de la tete − to cost a fortune. *Lit.* "to cost the eyes in your head".
 avoir des yeux pochés − to have rings around one's eyes.
 avoir des yeux rond comme des piastres − to have eyes round like saucers.
 avoir des yeux tout le tour de la tête − to have eyes in the back of one's head.

Yinque : *expr.* − only. *def.* Il n'y a que.

Z

Zarzaille : *adj.* – idiotic, foolish.

Zézine★ : *n.f.* – penis.

Zigner : *n.m.* – *cf.* zigonner.

Zigonnage : *n.m.* – fooling around, stupidity.

Zigonner : *v.i.* – 1. to attempt without much success. 2. to fool around, to waste one's time.

Zigoune : *n.f.* – cigarette (butt).

Ziper : *n.m.* – zipper.

Ziper : *v.t.* – to zip (up).

Il faudrait ziper ton manteau – You'd better zip up your jacket.

Zozo : *adj.* – idiotic, foolish.

Bibliography

Printed Sources

Armange, Claire, Parlez-Vous Québécois ?, Éditions d'Orbestier, 2007

Bélanger, Mario, Petit guide du Parler québécois, Les éditions internationales Alain Stanké, 1997.

Béliveau, Marcel, Savoureuses expressions québécoises, éditions du Rocher, 2000.

Bergeron, Léandre, Dictionnaire de la langue québécoise, Typo, 1997.

Bertrand, Guy, 400 Capsules linguistiques, Lanctôt éditeur, 1999.

Corbeil, Pierre, Le Québécois... pour mieux voyager, éditions Ulysse, 1999.

Côté, Jean, Expressions populaires québécoises, Quebecor, 1995.

Denœu, François, French Idioms, Barron's Educational Series, 1996.

DesRuisseaux, Pierre, Dictionnaire des expressions québécoises, Hurtubise HMH, 1980.

DesRuisseaux, Pierre, Dictionnaire des proverbes québécois, Typo, 1997.

DesRuisseaux, Pierre, Trésor des expressions populaires, Fides, 1998.

Dubé, Gilberte, Dictionnaire des expressions imagées, Les éditions internationales Alain Stanké, 1998.

Dugas, André / Bernard Soucy, Le dictionnaire pratique des expressions québécoises, Logiques, 2000.

Dulude, Yvon, Dictionnaire des injures québécoises, Les éditions internationales Alain Stanké, 1996.

Durand, Marc, Histoire du Québec, Imago, 1999.

Forest, Jean, Anatomie du parler québécois, Triptyque, 1996.

Gazaille, Marie-Pierre, *Le Parler Québécois pour les Nuls*, Éditions First, 2009.

Gaborieau, Antoine, *La langue de chez nous*, Éditions des Plaines, 1999.

Guévin, Marie-Lou, *Les 1000 mots indispensables en québécois*, First Editions, 2011.

Gouvernement du Québec, *Le français au Québec*, Conseil de la langue française, 2000.

Keith-Ryan, Heather, *Quebec : Bonjour, eh ?*, Sheltus & Picard, Inc. & VOA Publications Reg'd, 1998.

Mansion, J. E., *Heath's Standard French and English Dictionary*, DC Heath & Company, 1939.

Meney, Lionel, *Dictionnaire québécois français*, Guérin éditeur, 1999.

Proteau, Lorenzo, *Le français populaire au Québec et au Canada*, Les publications Proteau, 1991.

Proteau, Lorenzo, *La parlure québécoise*, Les éditions des amitiés franco-québécoises, 1996.

Scheunemann, Britta, *Le québécois de poche*, Assimil, 1998.

Simard, Josée, *Comprendre le parler québécois*, Édimag, inc 2012.

Tétu de Labsade, Françoise, *Le Québec un pays une culture*, Boréal, 1990.

On-Line Sources

Angelfire

http://www.angelfire.com/pq/lexique/lexique.html

WikiPedia

http://en.wikipedia.org/wiki/Quebec_French_profanity

Printed in Great Britain
by Amazon